The Art of
PACESETTING
LEADERSHIP

KEYS TO GAINING THE LEADING ADVANTAGE

DAVE WILLIAMS

THE ART OF PACESETTING LEADERSHIP

Keys to Gaining the Leading Advantage

Scripture quotations marked KJV are taken from the *King James Bible*.

Scriptures marked CEV are taken from the *Contemporary English Version*® Copyright © 1995. Used by permission of American Bible Society. All rights reserved.

Scripture quotations marked NLT are taken from the *Holy Bible, New Living Translation*, copyright © 1996, 2004. Used by permission of Tyndale House Publishers, Inc., Wheaton, Illinois, 60189. All rights reserved.

Scriptures marked MSG are taken from *The Message*®. Copyright © 1993, 1994, 1995, 1996, 2000, 2001, 2002. Used by permission of NavPress Publishing Group.

Scripture quotations marked AMP are taken from *The Amplified*® *Bible*, Copyright © 1954, 1958, 1962, 1964, 1965, 1987 by The Lockman Foundation. Used by permission. (www.Lockman.org)

Scripture quotations marked GNT are taken from the *Good News Translation*®. Copyright © 1992. Used by permission of American Bible Society. All rights reserved.

Copyright © 2014 by Dr. David R. Williams
Cover design by Kristy Prince
Illustrations by Dennis Preston

Soft Cover Edition: ISBN 978162-985012-2
Hard Cover Edition: ISBN 978162-985013-9

DECAPOLIS
PUBLISHING

Lansing, Michigan
www.decapolisbooks.com
Printed in the United States of America

Books by Dave Williams

ABC's of Success and Happiness
Angels: They are Watching You
Beatitudes: Success 101
The Beauty of Holiness
Coming Into the Wealthy Place
The Desires of Your Heart
Developing the Spirit of a Conqueror
Elite Prayer Warriors
Emerging Leaders
End-Times Bible Prophecy
Filled
Genuine Prosperity
Gifts that Shape Your Life and Change Your World
Have You Heard from the Lord Lately?
How to Be a High Performance Believer
How to Help Your Pastor Succeed
The Jezebel Spirit
Miracle Breakthrough Power of the First Fruit
The Miracle of Faith Goals
Miracle Results of Fasting
The New Life...The Start of Something Wonderful
Pacesetting Leadership
The Pastor's Pay
The Presence of God
Private Garden
Radical Fasting
Radical Forgiveness
Radical Healing
Regaining Your Spiritual Momentum
The Road to Radical Riches
Seven Sign Posts on the Road to Spiritual Maturity
Skill for Battle: The Art of Spiritual Warfare
Somebody Out There Needs You
Toxic Committees and Venomous Boards
What to Do if You Miss the Rapture
The World Beyond
Your Pastor: A Key to Your Personal Wealth
Your Spectacular Mind

Dedication

This book is dedicated to my successor, my pastor, and my friend
—a true pacesetting leader for the third millennium—
Reverend Kevin Berry.

TABLE OF CONTENTS

"God has given you a call and a destiny. He has created you to be a pacesetting leader, more than a winner, through Jesus Christ, our Lord."

~Dave Williams

"...Today I will begin to make you a great leader in the eyes of all....They will know that I am with you...."

~Joshua 3:7b NLT

WELCOME TO PACESETTING LEADERSHIP

Get ready to launch your life into a fresh dimension!

You are about to embark on one of the greatest endeavors of your life—becoming a pacesetting leader in whatever you are called to do. The principles in this book will advance your life, and the lives of everyone around you, to greater levels of achievement as you begin to experience and practice the art of pacesetting leadership. I have watched these principles transform lives, businesses, and ministries for several decades—and they will transform your life and your calling as you put them into action.

At whatever level of leadership you are starting, these principles carry the power to launch you years ahead. They are tried and true; they come straight from the Bible, and they work. Readers naturally come to this book with varying degrees of experience and confidence in their own leadership abilities. Some know they are supposed to be leaders and want to learn more about leading well. Many readers will not even recognize that they are called to be leaders in some area of life—so this will be their beginning. I want to assure you that these principles work for you at every stage of leadership. You can be a CEO or a new employee, a seasoned minister or a new mom. What you learn in this book will take you from where you are to where you need to go. Not only that, but these principles will provide a helpful resource for you to draw on your entire life.

FULFILL YOUR DREAMS

It has been more than thirty years since I started teaching *The Art of Pacesetting Leadership*, and I have watched as the principles proved themselves in every arena of human endeavor. I recently received a call from a man who participated in the leadership course and by applying those principles, fulfilled a lifetime dream to became a worship leader in a church. He told me that what he learned in the course has guided him for years.

Another man put the pacesetting leadership principles into practice and they spurred a business idea. Within two years of studying pacesetting leadership he sold that business for $2.3 million.

A woman who works in a government agency told me, "I bet these pacesetting leadership principles won't work for me because I work in government. It's a whole different world." But she tried them and was so successful that they created a new position for her!

Another man was promoted to a supervisor position even though he didn't have a master's degree that was a prerequisite for the job. These principles underlie success, no matter your field of endeavor or your present qualifications.

PERMISSION TO BE A LEADER

Many people wonder in their hearts if it is okay to aspire to be a successful leader. They wonder if they are simply proud or too ambitious. However, the Bible says emphatically "Yes! You are designed to be a leader."

1 Corinthians 4:16 KJV
Wherefore I beseech you, be ye followers of me.

1 Corinthians 11:1 KJV
Be ye followers of me, even as I also am of Christ.

Paul clearly and unapologetically called people to follow him as their leader. Also consider this verse in Psalms:

Psalm 37:4 KJV
Delight thyself also in the Lord; and he shall give thee the desires of thine heart.

If you have made Jesus Christ the delight of your life, then your desire to be a leader is not self-seeking. It comes from God. Being a leader will be a natural part of your walk with Jesus.

ALLOW ME TO BE YOUR COACH

This book is a step-by-step guide to help you become the pacesetting leader that God wants you to be. I have not met one person in thirty years who read this book, or completed *The Art of Pacesetting Leadership* course, who did not rise to another level as a result. Logistics, strategies, and leadership styles change, but what never changes are basic leadership principles.

With God's help, I am going to plant those principles of leadership into you so you develop the heart of a leader. This is the only leadership book I am aware of that doesn't tell you *how* to be a leader but instead helps to develop the heart of a leader in you. You won't just learn leadership, you will become a leader if you'll allow me to be your coach throughout this study.

Let's start with these words. Say them aloud: "God has given me a call and a destiny. He has created me to be a pacesetting leader, more than a winner, through Jesus Christ, my Lord."

Now, let's learn *The Art of Pacesetting Leadership*!

People who are locked into the status quo are not successful leaders.

1
CHAPTER

WHAT LEADERSHIP IS...AND ISN'T

God is looking for pacesetting leaders in business, ministry, homes, and communities. Right now, he is equipping leaders who can navigate through turbulent waters in this stormy world. We need successful, fruitful, blessed leaders to steer our nation, our cities, our churches, and our economy through challenging times.

YOU ARE CALLED TO PACESETTING LEADERSHIP

I believe you are one of those leaders. Pacesetting leadership is your calling!

At its most basic, leadership is the ability to influence others to change. People who are locked into the status quo are not successful leaders. Leaders are men and women who take people where they *should* go, which is not always where they *want* to go—at first! Through the influence of good leadership, people will follow in the right direction and expand their boundaries in the process.

THREE CHARACTERISTICS OF PACESETTING LEADERS

Why do people follow a leader? They are looking for three basic characteristics.

1: The first characteristic is trust

People trust you when they see your integrity, which means being integrated in spirit, mind, and body. When people observe the integrity in your life and leadership, they will trust you and begin to put you in charge of things.

2: The second characteristic is personal values

What will you stand for, and what won't you stand for?

3: The third characteristic is vision

We will talk about these three attributes in more depth throughout this book because they are the keys to fruitfulness in life and leadership.

Some people view leaders as men and women of ambition, focused on their own dynamic talents, changing the world by the force of their personality. True leadership is not about ambition, dynamic talents, or the type of personality you possess. Jesus, the greatest leader of all, taught his disciples something completely different. Among his followers, ambition took root, and one day they began arguing about who was the greatest:

Luke 22:24-27 NKJV

[24] Now there was also a dispute among them, as to which of them should be considered the greatest.

[25] And He said to them, "The kings of the Gentiles exercise lordship over them, and those who exercise authority over them are called 'benefactors.'

[26] But not so among you; on the contrary, he who is greatest among you, let him be as the younger, and he who governs as he who serves.

[27] For who is greater, he who sits at the table, or he who serves? Is it not he who sits at the table? Yet I am among you as the One who serves."

TRUE LEADERSHIP IS A PARADOX

Jesus Christ defines true leadership as a kind of paradox: if you want to be a great leader, not just an ordinary leader like in the pagan world, then you will do things upside down and backwards from normal. You will not focus on serving yourself and your own ambitions, but be entirely focused on serving others.

This may be the most important thing to understand about the heart of a leader: **True leaders have a servant's heart and a service mind-set.**

They are always asking, "How can I serve? How can I help and advance those under my leadership? How can I serve our customers or congregation? What problems am I qualified to solve for others?" Christian leadership seems to be a paradox because the leader is the servant. But it works, and in fact it's by far the most effective kind of leadership because it's based directly on God's character. It works in any area of life.

Look at the example of S. Truett Cathy, founder of Chick-fil-A®. He has 1,600 restaurants in 39 states, more than $4 billion in annual sales, and owns the second largest quick-serve chicken restaurant chain in the nation. He built his whole life and business on hard work, humility, and the biblical principles of being service-minded and servant-hearted. Without exception, every one of his stores is closed on Sunday to honor God. The business purpose statement for Chick-fil-A® is, "To glorify God by being a faithful steward of all that is entrusted to us, and to have a positive influence on all who come in contact with Chick-fil-A®." Imagine making that your mission statement!

When people picture a leader, they often picture a boss—maybe their boss or the stereotypical boss from television and movies. This guy has a big belly hanging over his belt and he walks around saying, "Come on, get this job done. The 'brass' are all over me and we're going to be in big trouble if we don't deliver!" Bosses who aren't also genuine leaders have all sorts of punishments and incentives to get people to work because they lack the ability to persuade and lead.

If that's your picture of a leader, you need to get out a big eraser. Just being in charge does not make someone a leader. A boss is a position, but leadership is a type of character that can be developed. It flows from the heart, not the position.

THE DIFFERENCE BETWEEN A LEADER AND A BOSS

There are many differences.

A boss commands subordinates, but a leader spends most of his or her time encouraging and motivating them.

A boss depends on fear: "If you don't get this done, you're going to lose your job." But the leader relies on people having a natural desire to do an excellent job.

A boss finds ways to assign blame for problems, while a leader looks for ways to fix the problems.

A boss tells people what to do, while a leader shows people what is ahead because of his or her vision.

Now let's move forward and examine more characteristics of a pacesetting leader.

DEVOTIONAL REFLECTIONS

1: What is your mental picture of a leader? Is it more like a hard-driving boss or an inspirational visionary? Or is it something in between?

2: What do you picture when you hear the words "the heart of a leader"? Do you see someone with overriding ambition and talent? Or do you see someone with a servant's heart?

3: Take a moment to re-imagine what a leader is. Meditate on the words of Jesus that "the greatest among us must be the servant of all."

Leaders are
made, not born.

CHAPTER

THE FOUR STAGES OF COMPETENCY

We all find ourselves in one of four stages of leadership. The four stages of competency in leadership are:

1: The unconscious incompetent

2: The conscious incompetent

3: The conscious competent

4: The unconscious competent

Let's take a look at each one.

The unconscious incompetent is the person who is presently incompetent in leadership but doesn't know it. How do you know someone is an unconscious incompetent? Just ask them! They think they know something about everything. You could describe them as clueless. They are the kind of "leaders" who command no respect and have no idea how to persuade or inspire people. Worst of all, they do not see how incompetent they are. They are living in la-la land. Many bosses fall into this category.

The next stage is much better—the conscious incompetent. This is actually a place of humility. If you realize that you are incompetent in certain areas, then you can take action and do something about it.

For example, I am a conscious incompetent at playing the piano. I used to sit down at the piano to play, but you never knew what I was playing! In fact, *I* never knew what I was playing! I had heard stories about the Holy Ghost coming upon people who would play without ever having a lesson. I thought, "Lord, let it happen!" It never did, so I remain a conscious incompetent when it comes to playing the piano. But since I know I'm incompetent I can take lessons and progress to the next stage.

That third stage is the conscious competent. You reach this stage when you are consciously focusing on becoming more competent in leadership. At this stage you are having to think about your leadership all the time. It takes focus, but you are growing more aware of your increasing competency. This is a good and necessary stage.

Stage four is the best place to be—the unconscious competent. At this stage you have the heart of a leader and are able to lead without consciously thinking about it. You might not even know how you are doing it—it's just in you. It has become a part of you. The goal is to become a conscious competent.

SOME ARE JUST BORN LEADERS, RIGHT? WRONG!

Many people assume that leaders are born, not made. I'm here to tell you the exact opposite is true. Leaders are *made, not born*. Leonard Ravenhill once told a thought-provoking story. A group of tourists were in a quaint village, and they approached an elderly man sitting by a fence. They wanted to know more about the history of the city. So one snobbish tourist asked the old man, "Were any great men born in this village?" The old man replied, "Nope, only babies."

No one is born a leader. Only babies are born. I'm a father. But I wasn't born a father. I'm now a grandfather. But I wasn't born a grandfather. I was a pastor. But I wasn't born a pastor. Like everyone else, I was just born a person. When I was delivered, the doctor didn't say, "Oh, Mrs. Williams! You've given birth to a pastor!" He said, "Mrs. Williams, you've given birth to a little boy!"

Leaders are not born. Leaders are made. In fact, *the word "leader" doesn't mean a whole lot by itself,* does it? You can be a lousy leader, a lame duck leader, an ignorant leader, an incompetent leader. It's the modifier that matters. Some people like to fancy themselves leaders, but nobody is really following them.

Once, our church had a resident shrew, a little gray mouse-like creature, who lived in the building. We made him our mascot. He wasn't afraid of anything. I would be eating my lunch and he would walk right up and sniff around. I would take a piece of cheese and feed it to him. When I wanted to lead that shrew around, all I had to do was take my pencil eraser, hold it in front of him and he would follow me anywhere I wanted to go.

I guess you could say I was a leader. But I was only leading a shrew. In the same way, if nobody is really following you then you're not leading, you're just taking a walk.

THREE LEVELS OF LEADERSHIP

I have studied leadership for over forty years now. In every conceivable profession or calling—business, ministry, education, home life—you find three levels of leaders. Each of us gets to decide what level of leadership we walk in.

1: First level—superficial leadership

These leaders are just on the surface. Often, they don't even want to be leaders. Their attitude is, "If nobody else wants to do it, I guess I will." Superficial leadership derives from title and position only. Picture a situation where the company puts the owner's son over a department. He has no skills and may be an unconscious incompetent. They can call it leadership, but it's not real leadership. It is puppet leadership, an empty position. God has not called you or anyone to be a puppet. He has called us to be *pacesetters*. Superficial leadership does more harm than good. It gives true leadership a bad name.

2: Second level—adequate leadership

Eighty-five percent of all leaders fall into this category. They are adequate at what they do, but that is all. If superficial leadership is on the surface only, adequate leadership is shallow. It accepts and enjoys the position of leadership but does not try to excel as a leader. This kind of leader does not study to improve. He or she merely gets by and is not really focused on serving others. This type of leadership is merely average and common in every sense of the word. These leaders shoot from the hip because they are ill-informed. You hear them say things like, "I don't know, what do you think we should do?" Or, "My opinion would be...." Everything is based on opinion or hunch rather than research and knowledge. This is not the kind of leader you want to be.

3: Third level—master level leadership

This kind of leadership will bring you before kings. It will give you a great follower-ship. It is the kind of leadership that will take you places that you have never been before in your family, your finances, and your ministry. This is the Jesus kind of leadership. It's deep leadership, servant-hearted leadership, extra-mile leadership. These leaders enrich every life they touch. They have vision. They are committed to excellence. They have purpose, direction, and focus. They have a special edge that keeps them going when the times get tough. They know what God is doing and they're becoming a part of it instead of shooting from the hip, dreaming up schemes and then asking God to bless the schemes. These leaders say, "God, what are you doing and how can I be a part of it?"

That is the level of leadership you and I want! That is the attitude that will turn us into pacesetting leaders.

DEVOTIONAL REFLECTIONS

1: In what area are you a conscious incompetent?

2: In what area are you a conscious competent?

3: Have you ever reached unconscious competency in any area of life?

4: Describe some examples of superficial or adequate leadership you have witnessed.

5: Now consider, have you ever worked under a pacesetting leader? How did that kind of leadership look and feel? Are you ready to become that kind of leader?

There are four stages from anointing to appointing, all important for launching from one level to the next.

3
CHAPTER

FOUR STAGES OF PACESETTING LEADERSHIP

Once you recognize that you are called to be a pacesetting leader, you will pass through four stages to be fully released into that leadership role.

Some people fail to become pacesetting leaders because they don't understand these stages. It's like baseball: to make a home run count you have to touch first base, second base, third base and then home plate. You can't just hit the ball over the fence and run back to the dugout. If you do, your home run will not count. The same is true of the stages of leadership. Pacesetting leaders move through four stages before being released into leadership.

THE ANOINTING FOR LEADERSHIP

First understand that the anointing for leadership is not the appointing for leadership. The anointing sets you on the path toward pacesetting leadership. The appointing happens only after a period of preparation. This is difficult for people to understand.

When you realize you are called and gifted to do a certain thing, the temptation is to start doing it without going through the stages of preparation and waiting for the appointing of God. I think of King David from the Bible. He was anointed to be king, but he waited fourteen years before he actually became king, and then it was just king over Judah—a mere sliver of Israel! He waited seven more years before he was appointed king over the entire nation.

In 1980, a young woman crossed the finish line in the 84th Boston Marathon. Strangely, she didn't seem to be out of breath or sweating. Was she a superwoman? Yes, because she was also invisible to the cameras along the route! They discovered that she had started the race with everyone else, then allegedly caught the subway and jumped back in the race half a mile before the finish line. Of course she lost her prize. That's what happens when you don't go through the proper processes and stages.

Anointing is not appointing. One comes before the other. You cannot do them out of order.

I have heard people say, "I'm anointed and called to be a leader in this area, so I don't need any schooling or mentoring or anybody to tell me what to do. I'm just going to start right now." They try to skip these stages and so they bring reproach on themselves and, if they are in ministry, on the name of Christ.

Think of walking onto an airplane and seeing a fifteen-year-old sitting in the cockpit. "Who are you?" you ask, and he replies, "I'm the pilot!" You say, "You're the pilot? Have you had any training?" "No, but I just feel called to do this." If you are sane, you will walk right off that airplane! The same with a dentist who feels "called" to dentistry but never gets any training. Are you going to let him near your mouth? Of course not.

FROM ANOINTING TO APPOINTING

1: Stage One—the anointing or the gifting

God has given you a specific calling, a purpose, whether it's in ministry or business or the non-profit world or in your family. The first stage is recognizing that you have such a gifting, something you can eventually do better than anybody else in the world.

2: Stage Two—preparation by study

The apostle Paul wrote in one of his letters,

2 Timothy 2:15, KJV
Study to show thyself approved unto God, a workman that needeth not to be ashamed.

The great men of God in the Bible were studiers. King David, as is evident in the Psalms, was a great student of God's character and ways. I tried to follow that example for four years when I studied under my local church pastor. I was his shadow. He took me under his wing. I knew I had a call, but I wasn't released into that call until I had studied for a period of time.

3: Stage Three—preparation by practice

If you want to become a pianist you can study the theory of music all you want, but if you never touch a piano, you won't succeed. You must practice! Jesus gave his disciples hands-on practice when he gave them authority to go out two-by-two to preach the Kingdom, heal the sick, and cast out devils. Jesus knew that the future of the Church depended on this rag-tag band of tax-collectors, fishermen, and country bumpkins. It wasn't enough for them to just listen to his teaching, they needed to practice. So after a time of learning, he said, "Now go out and get some practice."

I was a young pastor with a small salary. Back then people generally felt that the pastor should be the poorest person in town. My wife, Mary Jo, and I were living on $125 a week. Our house payment was $189.10 a month, and we were tithing double so we didn't have a lot to live on. When I needed a haircut, I went to the cosmetology school to let the students practice on me. It was cheaper for me and allowed them to get some real life experience. They practiced on me and the results were mostly pretty good!

4: Stage Four—release into pacesetting leadership

John Gallinetti was a member of Mount Hope Church who came to us from a Bible school and felt ready to be in the ministry. He had the anointing, he had been through some study and preparation, but he had not reached stage four yet. He was driving a truck, delivering cheese to pizza parlors and felt so frustrated. All of us have been there. We wait for a dream to come true or a promise to become a reality. We could tell that John had an amazing anointing for ministry, but he had to go through the stages. One day, I was in a Sunday school room praying and God spoke to my heart; *now is the time to send John to be the first pastor of the Mount Hope daughter church network.*

In 1987, we sent John and his wife, Wendy, and a handful of people to Grand Blanc, Michigan. They rented the basement of a parks and recreation building, set up chairs, and advertised with a sign out front with balloons. One by one people started coming to Jesus. Today, it's a mega-church of more than 1,000 members. They seem to be in a perpetual building program.

John told me many years later, "I felt like a little chicken inside of an egg trying to get out!" But he stuck with it and didn't rush to stage four because he knew that if he "emerged" too soon, he would not have the strength or character to carry out his calling.

Another man attended our church for a while and did the opposite—he wanted to skip Stages 1–3 and go straight to the appointing. I didn't know who this man was when he approached me one Sunday and said, "I'd like to teach a class here."

I said, "Why don't you take the membership course and *The Art of Pacesetting Leadership* course and let me get to know you a little better."

He said, "I've been on the board of three of the top churches in the city! Why would I have to do that?" Needless to say, he never taught a class at our church.

In the time between the anointing and the appointing, God has you in a state of incubation. He is transforming you little-by-little into the pacesetting leader he intends you to be. If you try to rush, you will find yourself not with an appointing but with a disappointing. Too many anointed young men and women have rushed into a calling only to fail because they did not complete the stages. That leaves scars on their hearts and makes them uncertain about their future in leadership.

Practice some patience and let God lead you through the stages of leadership so that you come out fully developed.

Next, we'll look at the key qualities of pacesetting leaders.

DEVOTIONAL REFLECTIONS

1: What stage of leadership do you think you are in? Stage 1, 2, 3, or 4?

2: Describe a time you felt frustrated with the stage of leadership you were in, and what you did about it.

3: Have you ever rushed into a position of leadership that was beyond your preparation? What were the results?

4: Take a moment and thank God that he cares enough about you to patiently prepare you for the amazing work ahead.

Pacesetting leaders stay on target with an unswerving sense of mission.

CHAPTER 4

MASTER QUALITIES OF PACESETTING LEADERS

Pacesetting leaders possess seven master qualities that build a solid character. I encourage you to study, consider, and embrace each one.

1: A positive, faith-filled attitude

It is unbelievable what attitude can do. I believe that at least 85 percent of success stems from your attitude. The attitude you want as a leader is one of great faith; an attitude that says, "God, I believe your Word. I trust in you."

I went to a hospital to visit an older man who had requested prayer. He was a member of another church, so I went with that church's pastor. The old man was in bed and we chatted with him for a while. After some time I said, "I'm going to anoint you with oil and we're going to believe that God will heal you." He said, "Yes!" I anointed him with oil, this other pastor and I prayed over him, then rejoiced and thanked God for the outcome. After that the other pastor and I walked out of the room, the first thing he said to me was, "I don't think he's got long to live." Talk about lack of faith! We had just prayed in faith, but this pastor walked away from that faith within moments. What a negative attitude! What poor leadership!

As a pacesetting leader you must have a faith-filled, positive attitude and keep your words in harmony with what you believe.

2: An unswerving sense of mission

For many years, I had a sign hanging in my office that said, "Stay on Target." You've got a call, a destiny, and a purpose but there will be distractions along the way. Someone once said, "If you're hunting for quail, don't shoot at rabbits. If you do, you just scare off the quail."

Pacesetting leaders stay on target with an unswerving sense of mission. Too many people get involved in things outside their calling when they should stay focused like a laser beam on what God has called them to do. These distractions can be tempting because they seemingly offer different kinds of "success." You might be called to ministry but working at a company that wants to advance you and offer you free college courses in their field. You have to ask yourself, "Is that going to help me in what God has called me to do?" If not, you must pass that opportunity up as a distraction.

When you have an unswerving sense of mission, you are like a river instead of a swamp. A swamp doesn't flow with purpose and direction but sprawls in every direction. A swamp breeds algae, bacteria, snakes, and other scary and unhelpful things. But a river flows positively in a certain direction and gives life to all sorts of beneficial things.

3: Seeks results, not activity for activity's sake

Many would-be leaders are hard workers, but their life is full of activity, not results. What counts is not doing *every* thing but doing the *right* things. Jesus had something to say about this.

John 15:8 KJV
Herein is my Father glorified, that ye bear much fruit; so shall ye be my disciples.

Better to have a tree with fewer, healthier fruit than a tree full of many tiny, useless fruit. Judge your activity by results.

4: Wants to serve rather than be recognized

The Pharisees and religious leaders in Jesus' day loved to sit in the most prominent seats at important events, loved their titles, and loved their position and authority. To them, leadership was all about having power over people and a big reputation. They were schemers and plotters. They had no desire to serve. Jesus said they wouldn't even lift a finger to help someone.

Matthew 23:3–4 NLT
[3] So practice and obey whatever they tell you, but don't follow their example. For they don't practice what they teach.
[4] They crush people with unbearable religious demands and never lift a finger to ease the burden.

Every business that starts with the main idea of only making money will fail. Every church that starts out with the idea of having the best reputation will fail, because every successful endeavor begins with *serving* others.

When I prepare a message, my goal is not for people to think, *Dave Williams is smart.* I have never been accused of preaching an "intellectual" sermon. Why? Because most people listen with one mind-set: **What's In It For Me?** Jesus knew this, which is why he talked to people in normal language and down-to-earth stories. He wasn't trying to impress others with his intellect. He wanted to speak clearly so he could serve his listeners. He essentially said, "Here's what's in it for you." He healed the sick, cleansed lepers, opened blind eyes, and fed the multitudes to show them a true servant's heart. In the same way, everything we do in life, church, or business should serve people without the goal of enhancing our reputation. As a pacesetting leader you have the privilege and responsibility of leaving your reputation in God's hands.

5: Delegates to and releases potential in others

Moses was on the verge of a nervous breakdown when his father-in-law Jethro said, "The thing you do is not good."

Moses was trying to be a good leader to two million people who were waiting in line to see him so he could settle their disputes and receive counsel (read Exodus 18). Jethro told Moses he was *not* being a good pastor because he was spreading himself too thin. Jethro then counseled Moses to let other people do some of the work; put some leaders over ten, some over one hundred, and some over thousands and let them handle the smaller matters. Then Moses wouldn't wear himself out. In essence Jethro said, "You will be able to lead them for a long time, and other people will get to spread their wings and become leaders under you. Everyone's needs will be met."

Jesus delegated responsibility to his disciples. Paul delegated to Timothy. It is the natural way of pacesetting leadership.

When I spoke at pastors' conferences in East Africa, they were very concerned when I talked about delegating because in their country the pastors did everything: weddings, funerals, baptisms, visitations, and more. I told them, "You've got to learn to delegate or your church won't grow." They thought I was a false prophet!

One pastor pulled me aside and said, "I do not believe you are a true pastor to say that we must delegate." I said, "If you don't start delegating, you're not going to live very long." At that time the average life span of men in his country of Tanzania was about forty years. I got a call the next year from that pastor's wife. She said, "I think you saved my husband's life. He's starting to delegate and let other people take responsibility for ministry in the church, and the church is growing."

Another young man named Cleophas said, "Pastor Dave, I did what you said. I started delegating and releasing leadership to others. My church has grown! We now have the only brick church in Tanzania. All the other ones are tin and mud."

Delegating expands your leadership and empowers others, which is a major goal of pacesetting leadership.

6: Commitment to excellence

"Good enough" is not good enough! I hear people say in the church and business worlds, "When dealing with volunteers, we can't expect too much. After all, they're not being paid." I say if they are volunteering to help, they deserve to be led by someone who expects the best! Who wants to volunteer for mediocrity? No, I expect a lot from every volunteer. They should be better trained and better equipped than many Bible school graduates.

God cared enough to send his very best when he sent Jesus. He didn't send an angel. He didn't send an animal. He sent his darling Son, Jesus, to die for us. He gave his best! We should give him our best in everything.

A good leader watches out for lousy workmanship. Don't do anything half-way. Do it with absolute excellence.

Proverbs 22:29 NLT
Do you see any truly competent workers? They will serve kings rather than working for ordinary people.

Excellence is speedy, accurate, dependable, and reliable. It's doing the very best you can. God doesn't expect perfection, but he does expect our best.

I'll never forget visiting a church where the pastor said, "Brother Clyde is going to come up and minister to us in music." Clyde walked up front with a guitar, unfolded a piece of paper (because he hadn't spent time learning the song) and said, "Well, praise the Lord everybody. I'm going to sing a song for you. Y'all pray for me though, because I didn't have a lot of time to practice because the ballgame was on this afternoon." Then he started tuning the guitar. Talk about lacking excellence! He proceeded to give a little sermon before singing his song. He rambled on and said, "You're going to like this song. It's got sort of a country flair to it. By the way, I want you all to pray for me because the dirty devil has returned to me in the form of hemorrhoids."

If I had been the pastor of that church, I would have shut down the sound, turned off the lights and whisked Clyde off the platform! How could he put that lazy, undisciplined servant in front of people? That was not ministry. That was pathetic. Pacesetting leaders must be committed to excellence and expect excellence from those they lead.

7: Has a proprietary disposition

Pacesetting leaders behave like they own the place even if they are not the boss or the owner. I mean this in the best sense of the word. The pastor, CEO, or "top-dog" shouldn't be the only one concerned about customers or members. Everyone in the organization should "own" the outcome.

If you see trash in the parking lot, don't say, "Where's the janitor?" Just pick it up! Make it your responsibility. That is part of a proprietary disposition. Take ownership of the problem *and* the solution. Then your business, ministry, or organization will rise above the others. You will develop in yourself, and others, the heart of a pacesetting leader.

DEVOTIONAL REFLECTIONS

1: In which of these seven areas are you strong? In which are you weak? Make a list, and rank these seven traits in order of your strength.

2: **Who are some examples of people in your life who exemplify some or all of these traits? Why do you say that?**

3: **What steps can you take to improve in your areas of weakness?**

There are three prerequisites of a leader, the first is a servants heart.

CHAPTER

SIMPLE PREREQUISITES OF PACESETTING LEADERSHIP

The ultimate goal of this book is to help you reach your greatest potential for Christ and gain confidence that God is building you into an effective, pacesetting leader.

Strategies change but principles *never* change. We are going to continue building on those principles block-by-block, step-by-step, and principle-by-principle.

RIGHT PRINCIPLES YIELD RIGHT RESULTS

If you don't build the proper principles into your life, you might suffer negative consequences. I read a story about Vinny and Sal, two friends who went hunting in the woods. Suddenly, Sal grabbed his chest, fell to the ground, and didn't seem to be breathing. Vinny pulled out his cell phone, called 911 and gasped to the operator, "I think my friend Sal is dead. What do I do?" In a calm voice the operator said, "Just follow my instructions. First, make sure he's dead." There was a silence. A shot was heard. Then Vinny came back on the line and said, "Okay, now what?"

It is better to make sure you understand the principles, or the results could be the opposite of what you desire!

In this chapter, we are looking at the prerequisites to pacesetting leadership. There are prerequisites to everything. Before you can go to graduate school, you have to finish your undergraduate work. Before you do your undergraduate work, you must have a high school diploma.

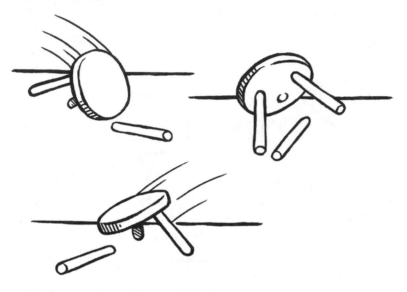

In the same way, there are prerequisites to pacesetting leadership. These prerequisites are like the legs of a three-legged stool. You know that a one-legged stool or even a two-legged stool won't work. It takes three legs for a stool to stand securely. In the same way, pacesetting leadership has three legs that must be in place for it to work. They are:

1: A servant's heart

2: A teachable attitude

3: A desire to draw ever closer to Jesus

If any one of these foundational principles are absent, pacesetting leadership will fail.

When I interview people to hire for my staff, I always ask myself, "Does he or she have a servant's heart? Is he or she teachable or does he or she know it all already? And does he or she have a desire to ever draw closer to Jesus, which keeps motivations proper?" There are different styles of leadership, but with these three prerequisites built into your heart, your leadership will stand the test of time.

A SERVANT'S HEART

Let's look at the first leg of the stool—a servant's heart.

Mark 9:33–35 NLT

[33] After they arrived at Capernaum and settled in a house, Jesus asked his disciples, "What were you discussing out on the road?"

[34] But they didn't answer, because they had been arguing about which of them was the greatest.

[35] He sat down, called the twelve disciples over to him, and said, "Whoever wants to be first must take last place and be the servant of everyone else."

Notice that Jesus did not rebuke them for wanting to be great! Essentially, he said, "You can be great, but the path to greatness begins with being servant-hearted and service-minded." You can't be great without becoming a servant.

"The measure of a man is not in how many servants he has, but how many he serves."

~D. L. Moody

JESUS—SERVANT HERO

Years ago, I was fascinated to watch an interview on television of a young businessman who was a hero of the business community. He founded a tea company at the age of nineteen. By the time he was thirty, his company was making billions of dollars. Independent tests showed that it was the healthiest, finest tea you could buy in America. The interviewer said, "You are a hero of business people all over America. Do you have any heroes of your own?"

This young man answered, "Yes, I do. The greatest hero in my life is Jesus Christ. He taught me how to serve people. He said, 'If you want to be great, learn to be the servant.' My goal was never to build a billion-dollar company. My goal was to serve people with the finest, healthiest tea on earth."

I wish every person I interviewed for a job said those words! I sat down with one potential employee who spouted, "I want to tell you something right now. If you give me this job, I will demand two days a week off and full health coverage." He listed several other demands. I thanked him for his time and the interview was over!

Jesus didn't call lazy, demanding people to be his disciples. He called workers! Notice that Jesus did not go to the unemployment line to find disciples. He found people who were busy doing something—fishing, collecting taxes, or working at some other job.

I interviewed another candidate for a particular position, but his ministry philosophy was out of harmony with mine. When we realized we had significant differences he said, "I'm sure over time our philosophies will blend."

I responded, "No, they won't. There are three things I never compromise: my doctrines, my vision, and my philosophy of ministry. There will be no blending. If you don't flow under the leadership that God has established here, you don't come here."

PLANTING "SEEDS" OF SERVICE

A servant's heart is measured by a person's willingness to serve. A great example of this is Miracle House Ministry in Costa Mesa,

California. Teenagers would get together, go into a needy neighborhood and find a house that was rundown and overgrown. They would knock on the door and say, "Would you mind if we cleaned up your property for you?" They would do all the work for free; they just wanted to serve. Many people came to Christ because of their service.

They went to one house and a frail, elderly widow answered the door. She frowned and said, "I don't have any money to pay you." They assured her, "We're not here for the money; we're here to help you!" They washed her windows, did some painting and cleaned up the yard. Afterward, the woman was trying to get a few coins together for them, and they said, "We're not taking any money. We do this because we're servants of the Lord Jesus Christ." She started crying and said, "Could you introduce me to this man?" Right there in her living room she prayed the prayer of salvation.

When you plant seeds of service, God will give time back to you. He will make your way smooth and direct, and he will do his work through you.

I heard of a pastor's wife who was anemic and asked God for healing. She was taking iron and supplementing other remedies, but nothing seemed to work. Each morning she prayed, "God, what should I do to get rid of this anemic condition?" One morning, the Lord answered her prayer. He told her, "Get out of bed and fix your husband's breakfast." She whined, "But Lord, I'm anemic." The Lord didn't say anything else.

Realizing she had a choice to obey or ignore this command, she got up and fixed her husband's breakfast—much to her husband's surprise. He went off to work and she lay down again. The Lord said, "Get up and take out the trash." She whimpered, "But Lord, I'm too tired. I'm anemic!" The Lord didn't respond. So she got the trash together and took it to the curb. For the next few hours, God just kept giving her more jobs. By noon she realized she didn't feel tired. She was totally healed.

God opened doors of ministry to her and she started speaking to women all over America. Her miracle began when God told her, "Serve your husband."

HOW TO SERVE WELL

1: Serve in a way that does not draw attention

Matthew 6:1–4 MSG

[1] "Be especially careful when you are trying to be good so that you don't make a performance out of it. It might be good theater, but the God who made you won't be applauding.

[2-4] "When you do something for someone else, don't call attention to yourself. You've seen them in action, I'm sure— 'playactors' I call them—treating prayer meeting and street corner alike as a stage, acting compassionate as long as someone is watching, playing to the crowds. They get applause, true, but that's all they get. When you help someone out, don't think about how it looks. Just do it—quietly and unobtrusively. That is the way your God, who conceived you in love, working behind the scenes, helps you out."

Jesus said to serve in a way that doesn't draw attention to yourself. I've seen people who make one hospital visit and brag to everybody, "I went up and saw Charlie in the hospital. I had a lot of other things to do, but I fit it into my schedule." They draw attention to themselves. Pacesetting leaders believe that God sees when they serve, and that he gives the rewards. Serve for God, not for what you might get from it.

2: Serve in a way that you can

God does not require you to serve beyond your calling or abilities. He uses what you have and who you are. In the Gospel of Mark, a woman anointed Jesus with costly oil. The disciples were upset that she had "wasted" such valuable oil on a display of love for Jesus, instead of selling it for money for the poor.

Mark 14:6–9 MSG

6–9 But Jesus said, "Let her alone. Why are you giving her a hard time? She has just done something wonderfully significant for me. You will have the poor with you every day for the rest of your lives. Whenever you feel like it, you can do something for them. Not so with me. She did what she could when she could—she pre-anointed my body for burial. And you can be sure that wherever in the whole world the Message is preached, what she just did is going to be talked about admiringly."

Service is doing what you can when you can with what you have. This woman wasn't expected to do what she could not do—and neither are you! Serve in a way you can. Recognize what you can do, and what you are less capable of doing, then do what you can do.

Everybody fits somewhere, but nobody fits everywhere. If you are not an artist and somebody asks you to paint a mural on their wall, it is perfectly okay to say, "I'm not likely to do that very well. You might want to get someone a little more qualified."

Years ago I felt guilty morning, noon, and night because I never measured up to what people thought I should be as a pastor. It took four years before I finally threw in the towel and said, "I don't care what people think anymore. I'm casting my care on Jesus. I'm going to do what I can do, and that's all I can do."

That was a huge hurdle for me to overcome on the path to becoming a pacesetting leader, but it relieved me of a huge burden. I suggest you do the same.

3: Serve faithfully

Matthew 25:21 AMP

His master said to him, Well done, you upright (honorable, admirable) and faithful servant! You have been faithful and

> trustworthy over a little; I will put you in charge of much.
> Enter into and share the joy (the delight, the blessedness)
> which your master enjoys.

God adds to our responsibility as we serve faithfully with the little we have. The key word here is *faithful.*

Have you ever wondered why the Bible says "many are called, but few are chosen"? I found the idea that connects the calling and the choosing in Revelations.

> **Revelation 17:14 NLT** [emphasis added]
> "Together they will go to war against the Lamb, but the
> Lamb will defeat them because he is Lord of all lords and
> King of all kings. And his *called and chosen and faithful* ones
> will be with him."

Faithfulness is the bridge between the calling and the choosing. Some are chosen to pastor mega-churches and win thousands of people to Christ, but they never actually do it because they haven't been faithful with the small things God gave them to do first.

Business grows when the business is faithful in small things: customer service, good employee management, fair pay and benefits. Those small things create the bridge from little to big, good to great, called to chosen.

Being faithful means living by God's values in whatever you do. The quality of your materials will determine the quality of what you build. You can't build a marble temple out of mud and manure.

In 1975, the Securities Exchange Commission uncovered a $2.5 million bribe an American businessman took from Honduras in return for that government reducing taxes on banana exports. His company exported bananas from Honduras. Weeks later, when he realized he was facing indictment, he went to the forty-fourth floor of the Pan Am Building in Manhattan and, with his briefcase in his hand, ran through the window and fell to his death.[1] He built with bad materials and his "house" came crashing down. He was not faithful. You do the opposite and be servant-hearted no matter how big your area of service.

DEVOTIONAL REFLECTIONS

1: In what area are you serving others now?

2: What was the most enjoyable time of service you have had? Why was it enjoyable?

3: What do you find difficult about serving others?

4: Ask God to put in you the heart of a true servant like Jesus.

---

[1] www.thehallofinfamy.org/inductees. php?action=detail&artist= eli_black

There are three prerequisites to Christian leadership.

CHAPTER 6

TEACHABILITY & DRAWING CLOSER

PREREQUISITE TWO: A TEACHABLE ATTITUDE

This means listening and learning. Jesus listened.

Luke 2:46 NLT
Three days later they finally discovered him in the Temple, sitting among the religious teachers, listening to them and asking questions.

I have learned that when you're green, you grow. When you're ripe, you rot. People who think they are well-seasoned stop learning and start rotting.

Proverbs 10:8 NLT
The wise are glad to be instructed, but babbling fools fall flat on their faces.

Proverbs 10:17 NLT
People who accept discipline are on the pathway to life, but those who ignore correction will go astray.

Proverbs 13:18 NLT
If you ignore criticism, you will end in poverty and disgrace;
if you accept correction, you will be honored.

Proverbs 21:11 NLT
If you punish a mocker, the simpleminded become wise; if
you instruct the wise, they will be all the wiser.

Get the picture? Pacesetting leaders are also pacesetting learners! They take advice, seek wisdom, and are never "too big" to learn another lesson.

MISSING THE POINT

I knew a man who was so boring that everyone hated to see him come around. He talked about things that absolutely bored people. If he had talked about God's Word and what he was meditating on, what he saw for the future, what God was speaking to him, or even interests in common, people would have been interested. But he would drone on for hours about things that pertained to nothing.

One day he came to me and said, "How come everybody seems to run when I come around?" I replied, "Since you've asked, I will tell you. Brother, you are boring. You talk about things nobody wants to hear. If you want to talk to people, talk to them about something that's interesting to them!"

I gave him a little book that cost me sixty cents but holds six million dollars worth of helpful information. It's by Clyde Narramore, and it's called *How to Build Bridges to Other People*. He took that book and a few days later told me, "Praise God! This is the best book I've ever read! You know who really needs to read this book? My wife!" This boring man never got the message because he was not teachable. He didn't get the point that the message was for him. The second supporting leg of the leadership stool was missing so he continued driving people away.

LEADERS ARE READERS

As a pacesetting leader, it is your job to cultivate a teachable attitude. One good way is to read books. Not every reader is a leader, but every leader is a reader. I try to read at least fifty books a year. In my earlier years it was more like one hundred books a year. Every time I finish a new book I think, *There is always something new to be learned. What great lessons.*

There is always fresh revelation to be found. Taking in knowledge should make you humble. Teachableness is a mark of wisdom. We have to remain pliable and teachable. Some resent authority so they won't learn from anyone.

If you think you have nothing to learn, then it's probably not the teacher's fault that you don't learn—it's yours! When you become unteachable, you will have the dubious privilege of learning everything the hard way—through failure, pain, punishment, and embarrassment.

LEARN TO FILTER

Once, a man came up to me and asked, "Pastor Williams, if I join this church, will I have to submit to your authority?"

I replied, "I am the pastor of this church, so insofar as it relates to church issues, yes."

"How can that be possible? You are a mere a pastor—I am an apostle!"

I stated, "I'd prefer you go bless another church with your membership." His attitude was totally unteachable.

I am not saying you must be taught by everyone and everything, though you can certainly learn from both the good and the bad. However, you must filter the advice you get. Many people want to advise you, but they have no expertise in that area. I've had people advise me to make this or that investment because they have a "gut feeling" about it. But their own finances were a wreck! When I was getting married, one man counseled me that marriage is fifty-fifty. He told me, "Give no more than fifty percent, and make sure she gives her full fifty. Don't go fifty-one to forty-nine. It's got to be even." This guy had been married three times! He "blessed" me with his wisdom all right, but not in the way he probably thought!

Mark 4:24–25 NLT
24 Then he added, "Pay close attention to what you hear. The closer you listen, the more understanding you will be given—and you will receive even more.
25 To those who listen to my teaching, more understanding will be given. But for those who are not listening, even what little understanding they have will be taken away from them."

Listen to people who are successful and whose lives are fruitful, not spur of the moment types whose lives are not bearing fruit.

PREREQUISITE THREE: DRAW CLOSER TO JESUS

The third prerequisite for pacesetting leadership is a desire to draw ever closer to Jesus. Why? It's pretty simple:

Colossians 2:3 NLT
In him lie hidden all the treasures of wisdom and knowledge.

"...All the treasures of wisdom and knowledge." Wow! If a person is not in Christ Jesus, he or she has no real wisdom. Jesus has all the wisdom and knowledge you need to be an outstanding leader. If you draw closer to Jesus all the time, you will always have greater wisdom and knowledge.

When you lift your head above the crowd and determine to become a pacesetting leader, you will need wisdom and knowledge. You are going to face situations where there seem to be two right ways, two paths from which to choose. You know what you need? Wisdom from Jesus about which path is right. Choosing correctly determines whether you will fly with the eagles or scratch with the chickens. Wisdom will show you the difference.

PERSECUTION

You will also need wisdom and knowledge because leadership brings persecution. Jesus said,

Mark 10:28–30a NLT [emphasis added]
28 Then Peter began to speak up. "We've given up everything to follow you," he said.
29 "Yes," Jesus replied, "and I assure you that everyone who has given up house or brothers or sisters or mother or father or children or property, for my sake and for the Good News,
30 will receive now in return a hundred times as many houses, brothers, sisters, mothers, children, and property—*along with persecution.*

Any time you're advancing in leadership, you will experience persecution from people who feel like they are not advancing. When you raise your head above the crowd, there will be attacks and misunderstandings. That's when you need God's wisdom. David faced it; Daniel faced it; the early Christians faced it, and you will face it too.

Whenever you are a leader, not only are you the hero when things go right, you become the lightning rod when things temporarily go sideways.

I have received unsolicited advice from countless hundreds of people. "Brother Williams, our church is not going to go anyplace until we have more songs." "Brother Williams, I had a dream the other night. The Lord showed me that unless we sing fewer songs, our church will not grow." "Brother Williams, can't you do something about the temperature? It's too hot in this church!" "Pastor Dave, could you do something about the temperature? It's too cold."

So many think they can give you the key to success! Some are like Job's friends. They were quick to offer unsolicited and usually wrong advice. "I had a vision in the night, Oh Job...." Then they offered up their unsupported, ungodly opinions.

How does a pacesetting leader sort all these differences out? The answer is, you sort it out with Jesus' wisdom. And the only way you get Jesus' wisdom is by drawing close to him. Untold times I have been on my face asking Jesus what to do. I pray, "Father, in Jesus' name I need the wisdom of your Son. I need that wisdom and knowledge because I have huge decisions to make. I don't want to take this church down a wrong road."

Pacesetting leadership has prerequisites like legs on a stool: a servant's heart, a teachable attitude, and a desire to draw closer to Jesus. Make sure you have all three and are continually strengthening each one in greater ways.

DEVOTIONAL REFLECTIONS

1: Rate your teachability on a scale of 1 (the worst) to 10 (the best). How can you improve your teachability this week?

2: Do you feel a strong need to draw closer to Jesus? If not, what changes can you make to help you develop that kind of hunger?

3: What wisdom do you need right now from God? Take a moment and ask him for it.

Any time you're advancing in leadership,
you will experience persecution.

Authentic is God-made, synthetic is man-made.

CHA**P**TER

AUTHENTIC VS. SYNTHETIC LEADERSHIP

Now we turn to one of the most important decisions you will ever make in your life: Will you be an authentic or synthetic leader? This decision will transform your life and everything you do. It will determine if your efforts are fruitful or fruitless. This decision is critical to your success as a pacesetting leader.

Being authentic or synthetic means to live either from the perspective, principles, and power of God's Kingdom or the perspective, principles, and power of this world. John the Baptist said it this way:

Matthew 3:2b NKJV
"…Repent, for the kingdom of heaven is at hand!"

Jesus preached the same message.

Matthew 4:17 NKJV
From that time Jesus began to preach and to say, "Repent, for the kingdom of heaven is at hand."

These verses encourage you to live only the authentic way, from the perspective of the Kingdom of Heaven. Jesus spent a great deal of time teaching about living from God's Kingdom perspective. In Matthew,[1] Jesus started with, "Blessed are the poor in spirit, for theirs is the kingdom of heaven." He then gave parables about God's Kingdom. After Jesus was raised from the dead, the Bible tells that for forty days he taught the disciples about God's Kingdom.[2] If Jesus spent so much time teaching about God's Kingdom, it *must* be important! Understanding how to live from God's Kingdom perspective is the key to authentic living.

- God's Kingdom = Authentic
- Worldly power and principles = Synthetic

KINGDOMS IN CONFLICT

Some people are born again, meaning they are saved by the Blood of Jesus Christ. However, these Christians function in the realm of the five senses: what they see, feel, hear, taste and touch. They have not learned the difference between authentic and synthetic. They operate in the world's synthetic realm rather than the authentic Kingdom realm that is available to them.

Far fewer people are familiar with what it means to live from God's Kingdom, meaning his perspective and principles. Only God can give us authentic promises and authentic leadership! Man cannot create anything authentic!

John 3:6 NKJV
That which is born of the flesh is flesh, and that which is born of the Spirit is spirit.

Once while I was praying, I had a vision about the church I served as pastor that vividly illustrated the difference between

---

[1] Matthew 5, Sermon on the Mount
[2] Acts 1:1–3

authentic and synthetic. At the time, our church had many ministries but seemed to be stuck in neutral; there was no forward momentum or growth.

In this vision I saw a train on a track trying to move in the direction of God's purpose and plan. Sparks were flying out from under the wheels and everything was moving forward—but very slowly. I intuitively knew that this train was my church. My view of the train panned back, and I saw five engines on the front of the train. I thought, *with five powerful engines that train ought to be speeding along!*

Then the view panned back even further, and I saw three other engines hooked up to the back of the train. They were pulling in the opposite direction.

Then the Lord spoke to my spirit, *The five engines are authentic ministry and leadership. The three engines in the back are synthetic ministry. They represent people trying to minister in ways that are not a part of my plan. Their ministry is based in their own selfish desires, and they are holding back the church. You have to disconnect those three engines.*

Who wants to disconnect a ministry that looks good, sounds good, and is popular? No one, but I had to because they were holding the church back. So I asked the Lord, "How will I know which are the synthetic ministries?"

Again I heard God speak, *Don't worry, they will identify themselves to you. They will tell you that theirs is not a synthetic ministry.*

I spoke to the congregation one Sunday evening and said, "The Lord gave me a picture of synthetic and authentic ministry. One is pulling us in the right direction, and the other is pulling us in the wrong direction. We are going to disconnect all the synthetic ministries in the church. Everything that was born of a committee, a brainstorm, a good idea, or because we attended a conference and somebody else was doing it, is going to be disconnected."

I did not tell the congregation how I would identify the synthetic ministries, so after the service a woman approached me and said, "Pastor, I know my ministry is not synthetic, but if you want me to stop, I will."

I replied, "Okay, I would like you to stop." Sure enough, she left the church because she couldn't lead "her" ministry. She chose the synthetic over the authentic. This scenario repeated itself until we were free—at least for a season—of all man-made ministries.

God's Word is clear on the results of life and ministry that are not founded in God's plan:

> **Psalm 127:1a KJV**
> Except the Lord build the house, they labour in vain that build it....

> **Matthew 15:13 KJV**
> But he answered and said, Every plant, which my heavenly Father hath not planted, shall be rooted up.

> **John 15:5 NKJV**
> "I am the vine, you are the branches. He who abides in Me, and I in him, bears much fruit; for without Me you can do nothing."

> **John 3:6 NKJV**
> That which is born of the flesh is flesh, and that which is born of the Spirit is spirit.

All these verses point to one thing—the difference between the authentic and the synthetic.

HOW TO TELL THE DIFFERENCE

Everything that glitters is not gold, and the synthetic and authentic can look a lot alike. When I was a bachelor, I lived in a little 720-square foot house on a dead-end street. I worked an eight hour day at the power plant, and then I worked another eight hours on school and ministry studies after that. I had no idea how to decorate a house. My mother would come over and say, "You need to put some flowers around this house!" I didn't care about flowers. I would rather have put in gravel than deal with watering anything, but every time she came over she would tell me, "David, you need to get some greenery and flowers around this house. It would make it so much more beautiful."

One day I was at a dollar store and saw they were having a sale on plastic flowers, five cents apiece! So I bought forty flowers of all different colors, took them home, shoved them into the ground and within five minutes had a "flower garden." My mother drove by and said, "David, you have a green thumb and didn't know it."

Then the snow came. Mine was the only house in the neighborhood with flowers peeking out of the snow. From a distance they looked like the real thing, but when you got up close you could see that each one was exactly alike. They all had come out of the same mold. They were flawless and didn't have those little brown veins or ragged edges you see on real flowers. But they also could not give true beauty, a sweet aroma, or a tender touch.

The same is true of people who are synthetic. They look real from a distance, but when you look closer you find that they never admit any flaws! Authentic people are open about their flaws—they are living and real.

Most important, the authentic has the power to reproduce. This is the main test of authenticity: it bears good, lasting fruit. Synthetic flowers cannot produce anything. Synthetic ministries can only produce more synthetic ministry, which Jesus called "evil fruit." He said,

Matthew 7:15-20 KJV
5 Beware of false prophets, which come to you in sheep's clothing, but inwardly they are ravening wolves.

[16] Ye shall know them by their fruits. Do men gather grapes of thorns, or figs of thistles?

[17] Even so every good tree bringeth forth good fruit; but a corrupt tree bringeth forth evil fruit.

[18] A good tree cannot bring forth evil fruit, neither can a corrupt tree bring forth good fruit.

[19] Every tree that bringeth not forth good fruit is hewn down, and cast into the fire.

[20] Wherefore by their fruits ye shall know them.

Later in Matthew Jesus made the same point,

Matthew 12:33 KJV
Either make the tree good, and his fruit good; or else make the tree corrupt, and his fruit corrupt: for the tree is known by his fruit.

The Psalmist said this about the righteous,

Psalm 1:1–3 KJV
[1] Blessed is the man that walketh not in the counsel of the ungodly, nor standeth in the way of sinners, nor sitteth in the seat of the scornful.

[2] But his delight is in the law of the Lord; and in his law doth he meditate day and night.

[3] And he shall be like a tree planted by the rivers of water, that bringeth forth his fruit in his season; his leaf also shall not wither; and whatsoever he doeth shall prosper.

The difference between authentic and synthetic is fruit. Fruit is a *very* big deal to God. The first command God gave to mankind in the first chapter of Genesis proved this.

Genesis 1:28a KJV
And God blessed them, and God said unto them, Be fruitful, and multiply, and replenish the earth....

Jesus repeated this principle.

John 15:8 KJV
Herein is my Father glorified, that ye bear much fruit; so shall ye be my disciples.

It is impossible to fool people with your fruit because you reproduce what you are, not what you speak or teach. An apple tree can claim to be a pear tree, and may fool some people during the winter, but when harvest time comes everyone knows an apple from a pear. There is no hiding the outcome. A wolf in sheep's clothing can look like a sheep, smell like a sheep, walk like a sheep, speak the jargon of sheep, and hide among the flock for a little while. But when that wolf reproduces, it's going to reproduce a wolf!

SYNTHETIC VERSES AUTHENTIC

- Synthetic leaders love and thrive on the plaudits of man; authentic leaders thrive on God's approval even though it may not be popular
- Synthetic leaders draw attention to themselves: authentic leaders point to God
- Synthetic leaders seek "golden opportunities;" authentic leaders seek only God's opportunities
- Synthetic leaders gain strength from men; authentic leaders walk in the Lord's strength
- Synthetic leaders walk in rebellion, deception, and darkness; authentic leaders walk in submission and truth and their path is full of light
- Synthetic leaders appear to work hard with great amounts of activity that never comes to much; authentic leaders are always working toward a specific God-given goal or purpose

I have found that authentic leaders are usually persecuted by synthetic leaders. You see this in Jesus' ministry: the Pharisees and religious leaders were his enemies and found fault with everything Jesus did. They criticized Jesus because he was different. He operated from the Kingdom, while they operated by earthly principles of power. The prophet Jeremiah said,

Jeremiah 17:5 MSG
"Cursed is the strong one who depends on mere humans, Who thinks he can make it on muscle alone and sets God aside as dead weight."

Synthetic leaders are literally cursed. There always will be synthetic, man-made leadership, people who pulled themselves up by their bootstraps. But they only look good for a time, and then they disappear.

One year, on the Fourth of July, some friends and I went down to the riverfront to watch the fireworks. The first firework went up, and the crowd gasped in appreciation. Firework after firework lit up the sky, and I heard people around me say, "Isn't that beautiful? It's so impressive."

After the grand finale, the smoke drifted away to reveal moonlight shining down and a sky full of stars. For a moment, those fireworks were synthetic "stars" obscuring the authentic stars. But after the smoke cleared and the ash of the synthetic fell to the ground, God's authentic creation endured and shone forth even more beautifully.

Synthetic leaders come and go, ascend and descend quickly, skyrocket and plummet, fizzle and burn out. What you want is that authentic leadership based on Kingdom principles and the planting of seeds that Jesus causes to grow.

DEVOTIONAL REFLECTIONS

1: In your own words, describe what authentic leadership looks like.

2: Is there any "evil fruit" or synthetic activity in your life? How will you cut off that synthetic activity and become more authentic?

3: Right now, pray asking God to point out areas where your leadership is not authentic. Ask him to help you produce good fruit.

It all starts with a seed.

CHAPTER

THE LEADERSHIP SEED PRINCIPLE

The first principle of authentic leadership is that it always starts with a seed. In God's Kingdom, everything begins with a seed. The very first parable Jesus told of the Kingdom involved a sower sowing seed. His next parable was about a farmer who planted good seed and an enemy who planted bad seed among the good seed. The Bible says at harvest time the angels are going to come and separate the good from the bad.

Everything in Kingdom law begins with a seed. Everything that is alive and genuine begins with a seed. The mannequin in the department store did not begin with a seed. It was created by man.

John 12:24 NLT
I tell you the truth, unless a kernel of wheat is planted in the soil and dies, it remains alone. But its death will produce many new kernels—a plentiful harvest of new lives.

Seeds must die to bear fruit. In the same way, you must die to your own plans and ambitions to experience authentic leadership.

GIVING UP MY PLANS

I experienced the tension between synthetic and authentic in my own growth as a leader. I never really wanted to be a church pastor. My plan was to travel around speaking and teaching. I sent churches everywhere a full-color brochure including my phone number plus an audio message called the *Ministry and Teaching of Dave Williams*. Then I sat back and waited for the phone calls inviting me to come and minister. That was over forty years ago. I'm still waiting for one call.

Then Mary Jo and I visited Christ For the Nations, and a man prophesied over us, "Your ministry is about to change. Don't be afraid." He told me some of the things I would face in the months and years ahead. I thought, *that's kind of neat.* This man was the first prophet I had ever met; I didn't know there were prophets still around.

I got home, and soon the phone rang. It was my pastor, Glenn Snook. He said, "Dave, how would you like to be my associate?"

I said, "Well, let me check my calendar and see if I can fit it in." Of course he knew, I was kidding. My calendar was empty and this was clearly God opening a door for me. I eagerly accepted the challenge

The Lord spoke to my heart at that time, *Dave, your ministry has to be a seed. It must die.* I didn't have many speaking engagements, but I was on the radio in five states. When I traveled, I loved to listen to myself and hear the introduction, "It's time for the faith-building broadcast with Evangelist Dave Williams!" My show was on the same stations as R. W. Schambach and David Nunn.

My team and I also had developed a correspondence school for prisoners that was growing. But the Lord impressed on me, *Dave, you've got to plant your ministry, your dreams, into Pastor Snook's life.*

I remember the day I told Pastor Snook, "I'm putting my ministry on the back burner; I want do everything I can to help you make your leadership successful from this day forward." I dissolved my own evangelical association and donated all its assets to the church.

One day Pastor Snook called me into his office, put his arm around me and said, "Dave, I really appreciate you telling me that you're going to plant your ministry as a seed into my dream. But, I'm planning to retire in about a year. Every church I've led has failed after I left. I think it's because I didn't raise up someone to take my place. I'm hoping that during this year I can pour into you everything I've learned as a pastor; I'm hoping the congregation will select you as pastor after I leave. Then maybe this church will survive."

So, for a year I was his shadow. One year and nineteen days later, I found myself the pastor of the church with 226 in attendance on Sunday morning and 125 members. I know that if I had not planted the seed of my ministry in the life and ministry of another man, I never would have become pastor. I would still be struggling out there trying to be what God had not called me to be. I would be trying to succeed in synthetic rather than authentic ministry.

For the next 30 years, I led Mount Hope Church. Through God's blessing and the work of a great ministry team, the church grew to over 4,000 local members, 43 daughter churches in the United States, 300 in Africa, and 200 in Asia with a combined membership exceeding 80,000. Would those ministry milestones have been accomplished if I had foolishly hung on to my own "synthetic" leadership plans?

How about you? Is God waiting for you to plant your leadership dreams somewhere so that he can raise your authentic leadership to greater levels of success?

You can give each day and each moment as a seed to God and your life will bear good fruit. Once, I visited a member of the church who had been working at a car dealership for seven months. On the wall of his office were seven "Salesman of the Month" awards. I asked, "How do you do that? Do you read a lot of motivational books and listen to motivational messages?"

He responded, "No, I get up before everybody else in the morning so I have private time, and I say to the Lord, 'How can I serve people better today? Help me be the best service-minded person possible. Send people to me that need my help.' Then I go to work, and the Lord always answers my prayer!"

That is how to be authentic in the marketplace. That salesman was a leader because he sowed every day as a seed, and God raised it to life.

HOW GOD GROWS SEED

After I became the pastor of Mount Hope Church, it grew into the largest church in the city and we began a new building program. Mary Jo and I had been married and living in our little house for seven years. We had two children, two bedrooms, and one bathroom.

We saved up $15,000 for a down payment so we could buy a new home. But when we were raising money for the new building, the Lord impressed on me, *give that $15,000 to the building program.* So we gave our down payment to the building program. Mary Jo and I said, "God's house is more important than our house. We can live in a 720 square foot home. I can work in the basement." We planted that money as a seed.

The congregation moved into the new church, and then a friend invited us to look at a house that had just come on the market. God sovereignly provided the down payment, and we bought the house and lived in it for twenty years. Do you think I want that $15,000 back? No way! I planted it and reaped a harvest.

In God's Kingdom law, everything begins with a seed. In Luke 16, Jesus said the way to tell if people are authentic is by how they handle their money. Do they tithe? Do they put God's house first? Do they put God first? Jesus said that if you can't be trusted with worldly wealth, he can't trust you with heaven's riches.

Luke 16:11 NLT
And if you are untrustworthy about worldly wealth, who will trust you with the true riches of heaven?

Some time later, Mary Jo and I made an annual pledge of $50,000 to missions—the biggest missions pledge we had ever made. We weren't even making that much money in a *year*, but we believed God would somehow help us to give that much. One day, I was browsing some company stocks on the internet and saw a certain stock. I felt impressed by the Holy Spirit to buy it. The stock was only twenty-five cents a share. I *never* buy penny stocks, and am an amateur at stock-picking, but I obeyed what I believed I heard from the Lord. I bought 10,000 shares for $2,500.

Two weeks later, I thought, *I should check on that company's stock and see how it's doing.* It had gone to three dollars a share! Immediately, I called my broker and told him, "I want to sell all my shares!"

Later, the broker called back and said, "Mr. Williams, I'm happy to tell you that from the time you gave me the order to sell and the time I was able to execute it, that stock went up to $3.50 a share!

Now I had $35,000. Minus the original $2,500 and the tithe and taxes, we now had roughly a $25,000 gain. I immediately wrote out a check toward our mission pledge. With God's continued help we later fulfilled our $50,000 faith promise. Our $2,500 seed had borne much fruit!

A few months later I attended an Assemblies of God district meeting and heard about a wonderful ministry opportunity to

Muslims in Kosovo. The Muslims were allowing their children to go to Sunday School, and then the children were telling their parents about Jesus. My district superintendent said, "I have pledged $5,000 to this program, and our secretary/treasurer has pledged $5,000 as well." I thought, *Lord, I suppose they're going to want me to pledge $5,000, too.* The Lord spoke to me right then as I sat in the pew, *No, I want you to give $10,000.* I asked God, "Where am I going to get $10,000? We just gave $50,000 to missions!" But I wrote on a piece of paper, "Mr. Superintendent, Mary Jo and I will give $10,000." I didn't have the first idea how it would be accomplished.

Soon after that, I discovered that a company I was working with had stock that had dropped from $50 a share to $16 a share because they had cut their dividend, and a lot of people on fixed incomes like a dividend. So, I sold everything I could because I felt the Lord telling me, *This is an opportunity.* In a short time we made $100,000 on that stock and we had the $10,000 to give to the Kosovo project.

A little while later Mary Jo and I were vacationing in Florida on a beautiful island in the gulf. I turned to her and said, "You know, this is the only place we've both ever loved. Let's see if there are any vacation homes available." There happened to be a Canadian couple who needed to sell their condo quickly. It seemed very undervalued to me. Mary Jo and I prayed and the Lord said, *Get it. This is for you.*

It made me think of the instructions God gave the Jews after they had defeated the city of Jericho.

Joshua 6:19 NLT
"Everything made from silver, gold, bronze, or iron is sacred to the Lord and must be brought into his treasury."

But when they defeated the next town, Ai, God's commandment changed .

Joshua 8:27 NLT
Only the livestock and the treasures of the town were not destroyed, for the Israelites kept these as plunder for themselves, as the Lord had commanded Joshua.

First the people of Israel had to be trusted with the seed. Because Mary Jo and I had been faithful to plant seed in the past, God allowed us to own that condominium and several other Florida properties from that point on.

As a leader, you have resources at your disposal. The principles of this world say to grab and hold everything you get, but a pacesetting leader knows that true success works in the opposite way: When you sow the seed God gives you, authentic, bountiful fruit will be your harvest.

DEVOTIONAL REFLECTIONS

1: **Have you ever grown a garden of vegetables or flowers? What did you learn about spiritual principles through that experience?**

2: **Describe a time you sowed money into God's Kingdom and saw it bear much fruit.**

3: **What is God telling you to sow now?**

Once you plant a seed, give it a healthy growing environment.
That means give it room in your mind and heart to expand.

LEADERSHIP SEED RELATIONSHIPS

When I was a pastor, many of the weekly prayer requests I got read, "Pray that God will give me a godly spouse." The principle of the seed works here, too.

HOW GOD GAVE ME A WONDERFUL WOMAN

I was twenty-six years old and unmarried, which was very uncommon in my mom's Polish and Czech family. Many of her relatives were married in their teens. My mom was married at 17. I would go to family reunions and my aunts and grandmother would say, "Hello, Davey. Are you married yet?" I felt a lot of pressure from my family to get married.

I wanted to be married, but I wanted God's will more. I would go to church, and when I saw a single woman I would think *could she be the one?*

I got so frustrated I went into my prayer room, knelt, and prayed, "God, you know I have a desire for a wonderful helpmate, but if I am more useful for your Kingdom as a single man, I want to plant my obedience to you right now. I give it to you, Lord. I'm never going to bring it up again. I don't care if I'm single for the rest of my life." Just then, a prophetic word came to my heart: *You will be married by next summer.*

Wow! Could it be true? I wondered if it was just the devil lying to me. Little did I know that at that moment a woman on a missionary trip to Hawaii named Mary Jo, a student with Youth With a Mission, was talking with her roommate. In the middle of the night her roommate sat up and began prophesying to her about her future husband.

God worked fast. A few weeks later, Mary Jo's dad became ill and she rushed home to Michigan to visit him. She and her brothers decided to stop over and see her old Bible study teacher—me. I heard a knock on the front door, and there stood Mary Jo. I saw her like I'd never seen her before, and she saw me like she'd never seen me before. She gave me a hug, and I didn't want to let go.

I said, "I'm leading a baptismal service this afternoon out at the Grand River. Would you like to go?" We went to the baptismal service, and then I gave her a ride home.

She graduated from Bible school a few months later, and we started dating. We would talk on the phone until 3:00 a.m. One evening we were sitting in the parking lot of a restaurant. I looked at her and said, "You know what?"

She said, "Yeah, I know, but I want you to ask me anyway." So we were married June 3, 1978, two and a half weeks before the official start of summer. How did I get a perfect wife? I planted the seed of my desire for a helpmate and God made it happen.

HOW TO GROW A SEED

Once you plant a seed, give it a healthy growing environment. That means give it room in your mind and heart to expand.

Goldfish in a little bowl stay little. Goldfish in a big pond grow huge! It's the same with every living thing: we grow to fit our environment. So it is with your seeds. They will stay small, unless you give them space to develop.

I had a pastor friend whose church was rapidly growing. People had to sit on the floor because it was growing so fast. Supernatural growth is great, but you've got to give people a place to park, a place to sit, learning space, and a place to thrive. If you don't, growth will be stunted.

Instead of making plans to move into another building, or start a building program to accommodate all this growth, my friend stubbornly stayed put. The pressure of growth became too great, and some in the church broke off and started another church to give people a bigger environment for growing in their faith.

A business can have the same problem. If there is not enough manpower or capacity to handle the workload, customers will become dissatisfied and the business will stop thriving and eventually die.

It's a good idea to start building or planning before you hit your capacity. I know a pastor who added 200 parking spaces, and then his church grew by 600 people!

Another way we give seeds a proper growing environment is to speak and act in support of them. Don't say, "Maybe I was wrong. This seed is not going to grow. It looks dead." Rather, support it by saying, "I believe and am convinced that this seed will grow because that is what God promised." Then look to Jesus Christ as the source of all growth. He provides the soil, the nutrients, and the water.

Always ask, "Is this a human idea? Is this God's idea? Am I trying to build a personal empire, or am I more concerned about the Kingdom of God?" If the idea truly came from God, then speak and act in support of God's authentic fruitfulness.

DEVOTIONAL REFLECTIONS

1: Are there any relationships or desires you need to plant to God and let die to self? Name them.

2: What can you do today to give your seeds a proper environment for growth? What can you speak to them?

3: Do you have a testimony of planting a seed desire in the past and seeing it take new life? Describe that experience briefly.

4: Ask God, "Is there anything I need to plant as a seed so that it can grow authentically?"

Always ask, "Is this a human idea?
Is this God's idea?"

God isn't looking for perfect people, he is looking for
people with perfect hearts toward him.

10

A PERFECT LEADER?

A newly married, foolish husband said to his bride, "Darling, now that we're married, I'd like to tell you about some of your flaws. Do you mind?"

She replied, "I don't mind in the least. It was those very flaws that caused me not to get a better husband than you."

Ouch! The Bible says,

Leviticus 11:44a NLT
For I am the Lord your God. You must consecrate yourselves and be holy, because I am holy.

Jesus said,

Matthew 5:48 NKJV
Therefore you shall be perfect, just as your Father in heaven is perfect.

Many people want to wait until they are perfect to become a leader. They say, "I don't have what it takes to do the task because I'm not perfect enough!" But I made an amazing and liberating discovery: God is not looking for perfect people. He is looking for people with *perfect hearts toward him.* When Jesus said to be perfect as your heavenly Father is perfect, he meant growing into complete maturity of godliness in mind and character, reaching the highest level of virtue and integrity.

PERFECT MEANS GROWING.

No leader is perfect. You can take relief in knowing that you, or any other person, will never arrive at perfection. Great leaders have leaps of faith and lapses of faith. Take Noah, for example. He was called perfect, but he got drunk after the flood. Abraham, the father of faith, let his wife go with another man because he was afraid. Job was called perfect, but God rebuked him strongly for what Job said. David, a man after God's heart, committed a terrible sin and covered it up with an even worse sin. None of Jesus' disciples were perfect. James and John wanted to call fire down out of heaven on people who would not receive Jesus' message. Peter was filled with the Holy Spirit, but he still made many mistakes as recorded in the Gospels and the book of Acts.

You can find such examples of "leaps and lapses" through the entire Bible. Yet David wrote,

> **Psalm 101:2 NKJV**
> I will behave wisely in a perfect way. Oh, when will You come to me? I will walk within my house with a perfect heart.

What does this mean, a "perfect way"? There are three keys to what God means by having a "perfect" heart and how to be a perfect pacesetting leader.

FIRST KEY: SURRENDERED HEART

A perfect heart is first a surrendered heart. You know you have a surrendered heart when you say, "God, I'll do it your way and not my way." When Moses came upon the burning bush the Lord said, "Take your sandals off your feet, for the place where you stand is holy ground."[1] Do you think God told Moses to take off his shoes because his bare feet were somehow cleaner or more holy? No, here Moses' shoes are symbolic of human plans.

Moses had tried to deliver the children of Israel in his own power and his own way. Now God said, "Take off your shoes, sacrifice the 'seed' of your own plans and start doing it my way." When Moses finally surrendered to God's will, the Lord was able to use him mightily! When you surrender to God, he will use you mightily, too.

Singer Mike Adkins helped us dedicate our 3,000 seat worship center back in 1987. He has a great story of surrender. His records weren't selling very well, so he prayed and asked God to give him more success. One day Mike looked out his window and saw "old Norman" across the street. Nobody in the neighborhood liked Norman. He didn't understand personal hygiene, so they said he smelled bad. He always said, "Yup, yup, yup," and didn't act "normal" like other people. People called him "weird."

One day, Mike saw Norman trying to start his lawn mower. The Lord spoke to Mike, *Go help him start his lawn mower.*

Mike protested, "Oh, Lord! If I go over and help him start his lawn mower, he's going to want to talk to me. He smells, and he's strange." The Lord didn't answer, so Mike went across the street to help Norman start the lawn mower.

After that the Lord said, *Invite him over to your house to watch The 700 Club on television.*

Mike said, "Lord, if I invite him over to my house, he's going to want to sit in my chair. If he sits in my chair, my chair's going to stink!" The Lord didn't respond, so Mike said, "Norman, do you want to come over to my house and watch **The 700 Club** on my TV?" Norman said, "Yup, yup, yup." So Norman came over and

---

[1] Exodus 3:5 NKJV

plopped down in Mike's favorite chair. When the program was over, the Lord said to Mike, *Ask Norman if he'd like to know me.*

Mike asked, "Norman, would you like to know Jesus?" Norman said he would. Right there in Mike's living room, Norman received Jesus as his Savior.

The Lord wasn't done. He said, *Mike, go over to Norman's house and clean it.* Norman's house looked like it had *never* been cleaned. Mike had to use putty knives to scrape the goo off the floor in the bathroom.

Then the Lord said, *Now, teach Norman about hygiene.* So Mike taught Norman hygiene. The Lord said, *Take Norman to the dentist and get his teeth fixed.* Mike kept listening and obeying the Lord.

He learned that Norman's mother had died when he was just a kid, and his dad was killed in a mining accident. Norman had been left to raise himself. Norman and Mike became good friends and started going to get ice cream cones together once a week.

But something else happened. All of a sudden, one of the national Christian television networks invited Mike to be a guest on one of their programs. The Lord spoke to the network owner's heart, *I want you to give Mike a free half-hour program every week.* Mike went from speaking in little churches and meetings to national prominence overnight. His recordings became top sellers. He wrote a hit song called, *Norman, Jesus Loves You.* His obedience to God with Norman seemed totally unrelated to record sales. But God was looking for a surrendered heart—a perfect heart.

SECOND KEY: SURRENDERED LEADERSHIP

Dr. Paul Yonggi Cho was the pastor of the largest church in the world in Seoul, South Korea. I met Dr. Cho in 1980 in Orchard Park, New York. He had 80,000 members in his church at that time. When he retired, he had over 800,000 members. He had been a young Buddhist when an Assemblies of God missionary led him to the Lord. Cho started a church in Seoul and had thirteen members. He couldn't seem to grow any more than thirteen members.

Meanwhile, he was doing everything from baptizing to officiating weddings to funerals. His body began to break down and he developed heart problems. As he lay in the hospital, he heard the Lord say, *You're trying to be the "Great Cho." You're trying to do everything. Now do it my way. I want you to delegate authority and let other people also minister.*

That was contrary to how churches operated in South Korea, but Cho obeyed. He told his deacons, "I've got to delegate authority to you. To make the church grow, we've got to do it God's way." They said, "Oh, no! That's what we pay you for!" Cho went back to God and said, "I told you, Lord! They won't do the work. Now what?"

The Lord said, *Ask the women.* So Cho called in the women and said, "I am delegating authority to you." They started leading small groups and the church exploded in size. Cho delegated so much of his responsibility that he could be away six months of the year training pastors in other countries, and the church still grew. He had a surrendered heart—a perfect heart, and he was willing to also surrender his authority.

The same thing happened at Jack Hayford's Church On the Way in Van Nuys, California. He couldn't get his church above sixty-five members. One day he was praying, "Lord, why can't I make my church grow?" The Lord gave him a vision of two trophies—one called "leadership" and the other "ability." Jack was trained in leadership and he had ability, so he was trusting in them. The Lord said, *Jack, I want you to give these trophies to me.*

Jack said, "But Lord! You've given me leadership and ability! Why do you want them back?" The Lord just replied, *Give them to me.*

"Okay. Father, I surrender all my leadership and all my ability to you. You build the church." In six years, it grew to 4,000.

The late Chuck Smith, my friend and a pastor in Costa Mesa, California, tells this beautiful story in a message called *How to Accomplish the Impossible.*

A church of twenty-five members called Chuck to be their pastor. They tried using clever ideas and schemes to encourage growth: "Bring someone to Sunday School and get a free goldfish!" They even gave out bananas, "Come and be one of the bunch!" Not surprisingly, these ideas didn't work. Chuck became so discouraged that he gave up and said, "God, I can't do it. You do it."

Meanwhile his wife, Kay, was praying and taking an interest in the "hippie" culture developing among young people. She prayed, "Lord, would you please send some hippies to our church?" Imagine a church of older folks in fancy dresses and suits and ties, and the pastor's wife is praying that hippies would come!

But a hippie did come. He was sitting on the curb when he heard the sound of singing in the chapel. It occurred to him, *I've done just about everything in life there is to do, but I've never been to church.* He wandered into that little twenty-five member Calvary Chapel church. At the end of his message, Chuck gave an altar call and the hippie came forward to accept Jesus. Chuck talked with him a little while and said, "Please come back and bring some of your friends next week."

The guy brought twelve friends, and they all got saved! The older people were having a fit. Those barefoot hippies were messing up the carpets and the atmosphere. But Chuck kept inviting them back. One man lived in a tree house by the beach. He nailed a picture of Jesus to his "wall" and started to light up a marijuana cigarette. Then he looked at the picture of Jesus and sensed Jesus didn't want him to do that. He never used illegal drugs again. There were countless similar testimonies from this time.

Those twelve hippies brought their friends and now there were well over a hundred hippies attending this church. Then they started writing new songs about Jesus, and that was the start of **Maranatha Records.** They started holding concerts and the church grew so fast they had to put up a tent to hold everyone.

That was the beginning of the "Jesus Movement." Thousands were baptized in the ocean at Corona del Mar in massive public baptismal services. There was teaching every night and literally thousands of souls were saved. There are now over a thousand Calvary Chapels in America, and 300 overseas, because Chuck said, "Lord, I surrender."

He learned that God is not looking for perfect people; he is looking for people with perfectly surrendered hearts.

In the next chapter we'll study the second and third keys to a perfect heart—the heart of a pacesetting leader.

DEVOTIONAL REFLECTIONS

1: Think for a moment—is your heart fully surrendered to the Lord? Are you holding on to anything that you don't want to give up? Are you trying to lead your way? Explain.

2: Pray and ask God to identify areas of rebellion.

3: List anything—an idea, a goal, a situation, a relationship, a person—that you have not surrendered and offer it now to the Lord.

Learn little by little, line upon line, brick by brick.

11

STUDYING AND STABILITY

SECOND KEY TO A PERFECT HEART: STUDYING

A perfect heart is not only a surrendered heart, but is also a studying heart. The apostle Paul wrote from prison to Timothy,

> **2 Timothy 4:13 NLT**
> When you come, be sure to bring the coat I left with Carpus at Troas. Also bring my books, and especially my papers.

Paul studied constantly. He didn't just study the Scriptures, he studied books by other anointed leaders. He wrote Timothy,

> **2 Timothy 2:15 KJV**
> Study to shew thyself approved unto God, a workman that needeth not to be ashamed, rightly dividing the word of truth.

> **2 Timothy 2:15 AMP**
> Study and be eager and do your utmost to present yourself to God approved (tested by trial), a workman who has no cause to be ashamed, correctly analyzing

and accurately dividing [rightly handling and skillfully teaching] the Word of Truth.

Paul also wrote,

2 Timothy 2:16 AMP
But avoid all empty (vain, useless, idle) talk, for it will lead people into more and more ungodliness.

It is amazing the number of would-be leaders who refuse to study. They may get everything else right and be authentic leaders God wants to use, but they won't commit to study and so they cannot advance in their leadership. They make it partway down the road God has for them and then say, "The study is just too much." Their leadership stalls at that point.

LITTLE BY LITTLE

God has designed us to learn little by little, not in one big gulp of learning.

Isaiah 28:9–10 NLT
9 "Who does the Lord think we are?" they ask. "Why does he speak to us like this? Are we little children, just recently weaned?
10 He tells us everything over and over—one line at a time, one line at a time, a little here, and a little there!"

A temple is built one brick at a time, and a pacesetting leader is built by learning one principle at a time through on-going study.

When I decided to learn to fly an airplane, I knew nothing about flying. The thing I thought was a steering wheel they called a "yoke." Every term was foreign to me, and at times I thought, *how am I ever going to learn this*? But I focused on it, studied, and earned my pilot's license in twenty-eight days. My instructors said I graduated quicker than any other student they had ever trained. Many times I wanted to quit! But I buckled down and kept studying. That is part of having the perfect heart of a pacesetting leader.

FUN WAYS TO STUDY

Here are some tips to studying effectively.

1: Find a special place where you can be alone

Create a sanctified space for studying the Word. I have what my wife calls the "Prophet's Chamber" in my home. In that spot is a reclining chair, a table for my coffee, and a collection of colorful pens and markers. Over my shoulder, a bright light shines down on my work. It's my sanctified holy spot, and it helps me get into an attitude of study better than just sitting at the kitchen table or in front of the TV.

2: Use highlighters in your Bible and books you read

Highlight important things you want to make a note of in the Bible and books you read. Don't be afraid to mark up your Bible and make notes in it. That is a good way of digging into the material and pulling out what you can use. You may also want to keep notes on the electronic device you enjoy using.

3: Buy a bunch of nine by twelve-inch envelopes

Proverbs 10:14 NLT
Wise people treasure knowledge, but the babbling of a fool invites disaster.

Envelopes or files will help you store up and organize knowledge. Mark each envelope with a topic you want to study. For example: love, faith, hope, endurance, patience, humility, and so on. Don't use more than twelve envelopes a year. One year I tried this strategy with seventy-two different envelopes and at the end of the year nothing was in any of them. So limit the number of subjects you study each year. Then begin to collect articles, CDs, Scriptures, and little books that teach on that subject and put them in the envelope.

When you feel like studying that subject in depth, or perhaps teaching others about it, you will have material at hand to dive into. It will be a great resource for you. This strategy has produced great fruit in my ministry. In one year I gathered enough material to help me write four books, teach for a year, and have reference material for years to come.

4: Number Four: Read! Read! Read!

A reader isn't always a leader, but every leader I know is a reader. Dr. Charles Blair told me he reads fifty-two books a year. I read 112 books my first year of ministry, and to this day I've always got several books on hand. Not just the "parchments"—God's Word—but books by anointed men and women of God and people from all walks of life. I read biographies of all types, books on business, Christian teaching books, and history books. I always find spiritual principles I can apply to my own life and teaching.

Remember, empty hearts are never fed by empty heads. Leaders should study to store up knowledge so they can bring out treasures both old and new for their students.

THIRD KEY TO A PERFECT HEART: STABILITY

Study leads to the third characteristic of a perfect heart—stability. Too many believers are changeable, up and down, into this and then into that. They operate constantly by feelings and emotions and zigzag all over the "mood map." One of the most liberating moments of my life was when I realized that my "feelings" should not determine my thoughts and actions. I don't have to check with my feelings before doing what God has taught me. This allows me to lead with stability.

Some people's impulsiveness and lack of stability prevent God from using them or promoting them. Reliability and dependability are much more important than ability. Ability is highly overrated. Ability without reliability is like trying to walk with a broken leg. Stability trumps ability every time. A surrendered heart leads to study. Study leads to stability, and stability means that God can use you in increasingly greater ways.

I knew an expert pianist who practices eight hours a day to maintain her skills and knowledge. She doesn't have the option of saying, "I don't feel like practicing today." Not if she wants to continue as one of the best. Neither do you have the option of saying, "I don't feel like studying this week," if you are to be a pacesetting leader. Eighty percent of the time, you won't feel like it. There will be something else screaming for your attention. But you must not become distracted, because studying is the right thing to do. Stability will be the fruit of your focus.

God is not looking for perfect people but for people with perfect hearts. Maybe you have felt useless to God because you focus on your imperfections. The good news is that God is not waiting for you to be perfect. He wants you to practice being a pacesetting leader right now! Surrender your heart, study diligently, and become stable. Over time you will develop the perfect heart that your calling requires.

Next, we move on to the attitudes of a leader.

DEVOTIONAL REFLECTIONS

1: **What books and articles are you reading right now? How many have you read in the past week? Month? Year? Make an estimate below.**

2: **What books and topics are you interested in taking up next?**

3: **What could you do to get more out of your study time? Create a "sanctified spot" for study? Start highlighting or collecting knowledge on certain subjects? Take practical steps this week to enhance and improve your study times.**

Reliability and dependability are much more important than ability.

Each person is a trichotomy of body, soul, and spirit.

12

ATTITUDES OF A PACESETTING LEADER

Business philosopher and radio personality Earl Nightingale called "attitude" the magic word. The late Zig Ziglar, motivational speaker and sales genius, said, "It's your attitude, not your aptitude, that will determine your altitude."

Attitude is a way of behaving that reflects what you think or feel. Your attitude will determine your success and probably the success of the people you lead. For the pacesetting leader, attitude is a foundation of success!

The next few chapters will help you develop the attitudes of the pacesetting leader God has called you to become. Ask yourself, is your attitude producing good fruit in your life? Is your attitude reflective of the Mind of Christ? Is it supporting your success or spoiling it? Let's run through an attitude check test. Have you ever said or thought any of the following?

- **"Some people get all the breaks in life."**
- **"Other people get the promises of God to work; I can't."**

- It's flu season, and I'm probably going to get sick
- All my problems are my wife's (or husband's) fault
- If I had a better boss, I'd be a better worker
- That's the way the ball bounces; whatever will be, will be
- If you're a success, you must be doing something illegal or unethical

The truth is every one of us has spoken or entertained thoughts along those lines before. But words and thoughts like that indicate wrong attitudes.

People with wrong attitudes downplay the positive. When someone gets promoted they say, "He was always shining the boss's shoes. That's why he got the promotion."

People with wrong attitudes magnify the negative. They say, "Did you hear about all the people who got killed in that accident?" The right attitude says, "Did you hear about the people who escaped death?" The Bible tells us to magnify the Lord, not the problem!

Psalm 34:3 KJV
O magnify the Lord with me, and let us exalt his name together.

People with a wrong attitude take everything in a negative way. You pay them a compliment and they say, "What did you mean by that?" People with a wrong attitude think in extremes: "He loves me!" "He hates me!" They have no balance. They jump to conclusions and misinterpret people's words.

People with a wrong attitude act upon their own senses rather than God's Word. They believe what they see, feel, or hear, not what is true from God's perspective.

Try as you might, you cannot change your attitude through the force of your own will. It takes the Mind of Christ in you to change your attitude so that you can look at a bad situation and see the good. Your first job as a pacesetting leader is to develop the Mind of Christ by allowing his thoughts and ways to permeate your thoughts and behavior.

A proper attitude is foundational to becoming a pacesetting leader. Thoughts produce a lifestyle and a life culture of either success or failure. The fruitfulness of any business, church, or organization will be determined largely by the attitude of the leadership. God holds leaders responsible. How can you develop proper attitudes for success?

THE LEADER'S RENEWED MIND

As a Christian, you actually have the mind of Christ which produces the attitude of a pacesetting leader. But some people persist in thinking only from a human point of view. They don't listen to Christ's thoughts or develop doing things his way in their lives. They aren't able to cast down imaginations that exalt themselves against the Mind of Christ. These people never become pacesetting leaders because they don't develop the right attitude.[1]

True leaders have the mind of Christ and as a result, everything around them grows and improves. Author and pastor Rick Joyner[2] has written a trilogy of books called *The Final Quest*, *The Call*, and *Epic Battles of the Last Days*. He tells of a dream he had of three armies of Christians.

The first army was the largest, but everywhere it went, the grass turned brown, flowers withered, and the trees no longer bore fruit.

The second army was medium in size, and where it went sometimes the land would turn brown and sometimes it would turn green. The influence was inconsistent.

[1] Williams, Dave, *Your Spectacular Mind* (2012), Decapolis Publishing, Lansing, MI 48917.

[2] Joyner, Rick, *The Call* (1999); *Final Quest* (2006); *Epic Battles of the Last Days* (2006), Morningstar Publications, Fort Mill, SC, 29715.

The third army in God's family was the smallest of all, but everywhere it went the grass turned green, flowers bloomed, and trees bore fruit. That third army was the army that was operating with Christ's thoughts.

Like the third army, you must develop the Mind of Christ. I believe it is impossible to be a pacesetting leader without surrendering to Christ and letting his Holy Spirit develop the mind of Christ within you.

When you said, "Yes!" to Jesus, your spirit was born again, but your mind was not. That's why the Apostle James wrote about the saving of your soul (mind) as a progressive event. Your spirit was instantly saved, but your mind and body were not instantly saved.

I have often thought how nice it would be if, at the time of salvation, everything about us—spirit, mind, and body— improved instantly. It would be nice to lose weight instantly, drop bad habits, and say good-bye to old attitudes and thinking patterns in a split second. But the unfortunate fact is, if you weighed 300 pounds when you accepted Jesus, three minutes later you still weighed 300 pounds! Your mind was the same, too. It still had thought patterns and attitudes impressed by this world. It was stuck in synthetic thinking, not the authentic thinking of the Kingdom.

Having a born-again spirit feels so wonderful that for two weeks after getting saved you're on a cloud. "I love everybody!" You think the entire world has changed. Then you encounter a trial or challenge, and the joy seems to drain out of you. You pray, you cry, and you wonder, "Why don't things change?"

It's because your attitude and mental patterns have been programmed into you and it takes time to re-program them. You were programmed by your parents, your peers, your teachers, your baby-sitters—the people you met influenced you. Their thinking became your thinking—even if their thinking was wrong. Research shows that attitudes are pretty much developed by the age of twenty. If you were born again after age twenty, you're going to have to work especially hard to kick out old ideas and habits and replace them with right ones.

Developing the mind of Christ is a lifelong process. This is the challenge to pacesetting leaders. You want to be fruitful and authentic in your leadership. You want to see your dreams and visions realized. But to be fruitful in God's Kingdom you have to know what God is saying, and you can't let his words get filtered through your old thinking.

God speaks to your spirit, not your mind. But often our unrenewed minds misinterpret what God is saying.

Many potential leaders and people of all kinds have no grasp of the wonderful things God has designed for them to create and produce and enjoy, because they haven't thought like God. They think like this present world. They are saved but their minds are not renewed.

1 Thessalonians 5:23 NLT
Now may the God of peace make you holy in every way, and may your whole spirit and soul and body be kept blameless until our Lord Jesus Christ comes again.

These were Paul's word to the Thessalonians. This passage illustrates that we are three-part beings created in the image and likeness of God. God is three-in-one: the Father, Son and Holy Spirit. Likewise, God created us to be a little trinity of spirit, mind, and body. The battles we face are in our minds—our thinking. The mind takes time to change. That is why attitudes take time to renew instead of changing instantly. But if you are to lead effectively, you must come into alignment by sharing the Mind of Christ.

When you battle old problems, it is never your spirit that's having the problem; it is your mind. The children of Israel came out of Egypt wealthy because God sent the wealth of Egypt with them. They had silver, gold, clothes, livestock, and much more. Suddenly, they were wealthy, but they still possessed a slave mentality. They thought like slaves, they talked like slaves, and so they started getting a slave's results. They ended up losing what they had—the opportunity to enter the Promised Land. Their outside situation was controlled by their attitude. The same is true for you. Your outer situation reflects your inner situation. True change comes from within, not from without. The Amplified Version tells us:

> **Ephesians 4:23–24 AMP**
> 23 And be constantly renewed in the spirit of your mind [having a fresh mental and spiritual attitude],
> 24 And put on the new nature (the regenerate self) created in God's image, [Godlike] in true righteousness and holiness.

> **Romans 12:2 AMP**
> Do not be conformed to this world (this age), [fashioned after and adapted to its external, superficial customs], but be transformed (changed) by the [entire] renewal of your mind [by its new ideals and its new attitude], so that you may prove [for yourselves] what is the good and acceptable and perfect will of God, even the thing which is good and acceptable and perfect [in His sight for you].

The *Harvard Business Review* sponsored a study that showed eighty-five percent of the reasons that a person gets and keeps a job is attitude, not aptitude. Aptitude makes up only fifteen percent. We all know it's easy and pleasant to work with somebody who has the right attitude. You can teach them aptitude and capabilities. But fixing an attitude can be a lot harder! It's ironic that companies spend so much money training people to have more aptitude. If they knew better, they would spend most of their budget on training people to have a better attitude. If you want the best company, organization, or ministry possible, work on getting your people to think more like God thinks!

Next we'll investigate some difficulties you may face in developing the right attitude for leadership and renewing your mind.

LEADERSHIP STEPS

1: Would you say you have a good attitude? Rate it on a scale of 1 (worst) to 10 (best).

2: How can you improve your attitude?

3: What steps are you taking week by week to allow the Spirit of God to renew your mind?

4: Surrender your mind and attitude to God, asking him to do whatever it takes to develop in you the mind of Christ and the attitude of a pacesetting leader.

Beware of difficulties and snares you might face in the process of changing your attitudes.

13
CHAPTER

DIFFICULTIES IN
CHANGING ATTITUDES

I have heard it said that in the business world five percent of people are super-successful, attaining much more than others. Fifteen percent are average in their success levels, just normal and not extraordinary. However, the greatest majority of people, eighty percent, are mediocre to failing.

I believe the same is true for churches. In the church world, only five percent of churches have over 450 members, and just a small fraction of those are mega-churches with thousands of members. Some people don't think they need church at all. They say, "Just go to the restaurant and meet with a couple of friends and call it 'church.'" Have you ever seen great or even good fruit from that kind of church?

Jesus said,

John 15:8 NLT
When you produce much fruit, you are my true disciples. This brings great glory to my Father.

Pacesetting leaders, churches, and businesses are meant to be productive and reproductive. Churches grow because growth is the nature of God's Kingdom. It's okay to start out small, but it's not okay to stay small. If you are born again, it's okay to start out broke, but it's *not* okay to stay broke; it's okay to start out with bad habits, but it's *not* okay to keep them.

It all goes back to the attitude of the leader. If the leader says, "Big churches are big because they don't preach the true Gospel!" they are going to stay small. If a business leader's attitude is critical and jealous of other businesses, I can tell you right now that his business will stay small. It's that simple. Your attitude determines your altitude.

There are some common difficulties and snares you might face in the process of renewing your mind. Let's look at them.

1: Lack of proper rest

Lack of sleep can mess with your unconscious mind. I got a call early one morning.

"Pastor, can you come over here? Something's terribly wrong with my wife!"blurted the man on the other end of the line. I went over to his house and saw that his wife was in a crazed state.

She kept ripping off her clothes while screaming, "I am Lucifer and I'm going to kill her!" The "her" she was referring to was her own baby! I thought she was demon-possessed so I prayed and bound the devil, but it had no positive effect. The Holy Spirit gave me discernment and I asked her husband,

"How much sleep has she had?"

He replied, "She hasn't slept in five days. Our new baby has been keeping her up."

We took her to the hospital and found that her hormones were all out of balance due to lack of sleep. She thought the rapture had come, she thought she was in the tribulation, and she thought my name was Wally (even though she knew me).

She was not possessed. Lack of sleep had completely messed with her mind. They helped her get some rest, and within weeks she was once again the wonderful, sane woman God made her.

Pacesetting leaders are not called to run at full steam all day long on very little sleep. That is a myth. God made sleep as a respite for us from our work. The Bible says that God gives sleep to those he loves (Psalm 127:2). Embrace that downtime and get plenty of sleep. Otherwise, as one general said, "Fatigue makes cowards of us all."

2: Weird behaviors

Using drugs, practicing mind-control techniques like hypnotism, or engaging in occultism of any kind can seriously damage your mind. Do you secretly read your horoscope? You say, "Oh, it's just for fun," but putting your toe in those waters means taking a big risk.

I knew a man who taught adult Sunday School. He started studying transcendental meditation, a practice of the Hindu religion. I told him he was messing with the occult, but he replied, "On no, it's totally non-religious. It's just something I do to help me relax." Soon, this great Sunday School teacher got the idea he was married to the wrong woman. He happened to meet his old high school sweetheart and "God" spoke to him, "That's the one you should have married." So he divorced his wife and started living with the other woman. Dabbling with the occult ruined his progress toward attaining the mind of Christ and brought reproach upon his ministry.

Some leaders are so fervent about outperforming the competition that they delve into dangerous practices like hypnotism, which they assert is a performance enhancement technique. You see magazine and newspaper ads that claim you can cure smoking and overeating, or make you a better athlete through hypnotism.

In simple terms, hypnotism loosens the wire between the unconscious and the conscious mind. The conscious mind understands and judges. The unconscious mind believes everything it hears. It has no power to discern or make assessments. That is why you must judge everything you hear. And you must not judge from a worldly or personal perspective; you must judge everything against God's standard, the Holy Bible.

The people of Berea where considered "more noble"[1] then some of the Jews and Greeks because they measured everything Paul taught against the Scriptures to prove they were supported by God's Word.

> **Acts 17:11–12 NLT**
> [11] And the people of Berea were more open-minded than those in Thessalonica, and they listened eagerly to Paul's message. They searched the Scriptures day after day to see if Paul and Silas were teaching the truth.
> [12] As a result, many Jews believed, as did many of the prominent Greek women and men.

Hypnotism sets your judgment and your conscious mind aside, which is an extremely dangerous practice.

Enchanting drugs also take you off track and even open your unconscious mind to satanic influence. None of these things have anything to do with developing the mind of Christ. They are incredibly harmful.

3: Negative self-talk

> **Proverbs 18:21 NLT**
> The tongue can bring death or life; those who love to talk will reap the consequences.

---

[1] Acts 17:11 KJV

This danger is much more common. Life and death are in the power of the tongue. If you are to be a pacesetting leader, you will want to get your words right.

Once I felt nauseated for several days. It finally dawned on me that I had been using the phrase, "That turns my stomach," frequently. When you say something, it influences your physical system to accomplish what you speak. I stopped using that phrase and the nausea went away.

A friend of mine felt her heart acting up, and she asked the Lord why. He reminded her that for the previous week she had said things like, "Oh, that breaks my heart." If the power of death and life is in the tongue, you ought to watch your tongue! When you speak you are feeding your subconscious mind, which will set up your system to do just what you've said. You might give yourself a heart attack!

HEARTACHES BY THE NUMBER?

The music you listen to goes into your subconscious and does the same thing, and you hardly notice it. I used to listen to an "oldies" station, but one day I listened closely to the lyrics. I heard things like, "It's a hard world to get a break in / All the good things have been taken." I never realized that's what the song said even though I had heard it many times. I shut that radio station off. No wonder people say, "It's hard to get a break. I haven't been able to get a job." What you speak goes into your subconscious mind and influences your life! Does negative self-talk help you develop the mind of Christ and a pacesetting attitude? No, of course not.

Some songs are beautiful but have an adverse meaning, even some "church" music. Once, a man in our choir sang a song with the lyrics, "He tells us not to worry, but we do." This song listed all these things we aren't supposed to do, but still do. I told the choir director to never use that song again. It seemed harmless—after all it was church music—but the lyrics lead to wrong, negative thinking and adversely affect our efforts to become God's type of successful leader.

DEVOTIONAL REFLECTIONS

1: What are you allowing to feed your mind? Are the words you say in agreement with God's principles or out of sync? Explain any problem areas.

2: Are you getting proper rest?

3: Have you dabbled with the occult like horoscopes, hypnotism, or the spirituality that goes along with exercises like yoga? If so, turn from them immediately.

Editors Note: See Dr. Dave Williams' book or two-CD message entitled **Your Spectacular Mind.** *Also available in Nook and Kindle editions.*

If you are born again, it's okay to start out broke, but it's *not* okay to stay broke; it's okay to start out with bad habits, but it's *not* okay to keep them.

Guard the computer room of your mind

14

STEPS TO RENOVATE YOUR MIND FOR SUCCESS

Romans 12:1–2 NKJV

[1] I beseech you therefore, brethren, by the mercies of God, that you present your bodies a living sacrifice, holy, acceptable to God, which is your reasonable service.

[2] And do not be conformed to this world, but be transformed by the renewing of your mind, that you may prove what is that good and acceptable and perfect will of God.

How can you gain mastery over those areas that have caused you so many problems? The only answer is by having the mind of Christ. The Bible calls it being "transformed by the renewing of your mind."

The word *renew* comes from a Greek word that means *totally renovate*. The only way to drive old things out is to push in new things. You don't renovate your house by adding new furniture, paint and decorations to the old ones. You must replace old the with new. It's not easy, but it is totally worth it for you as a leader and for the people you serve. Here is how to accomplish it.

1: You must be born again

By accepting Jesus into your heart as your Lord and Savior, you enable the Holy Spirit to work in your life. It's impossible to have the mind of Christ, or a pacesetting leader's proper attitude, without allowing the Holy Spirit to work in you. And he can't work in you until you make a conscious decision to accept the gift of salvation Christ provided on the cross.

2: Accept full responsibility for your mind

I have had to remove myself from certain environments and break off certain relationships because they were exposing me to wrong attitudes and unrenewed thoughts.

One person with a bad attitude can bring down everyone in the room. Likewise, an upbeat person can energize and uplift everyone in a room. Attitudes are contagious and determine the environment. You need to be aware of the actions, words, and ambiance of the people and situations you are exposed to. Be ready to remove yourself from toxic people and settings.

I read about a New York tenement building that was turning into a slum. Trash littered every area inside and out, and the building and halls badly needed painting. A group of Christians said, "Let's do something good for God and our community! Let's go fix up that building!" They raised money and inspired volunteers. They painted the building, halls, and windowsills, washed the windows, picked up the trash and landscaped the yard. That building was sparkling by the time they finished.

Three months later, the building looked just as bad as it did before the renovation. Why? Because the people who actually lived there had not changed. Their thoughts and attitudes concerning their living space were the same poverty thoughts that had caused the problem in the first place. Their outer reality reflected their unchanged inner reality.

You can outwardly change residences, churches, jobs, pastors, people or anything else. But unless the change comes from a change in thinking or a change of heart—until the change comes from the inside—the change will not last.

A woman in Chicago experienced a different situation. She lived in a city-owned building that had become a run-down slum. She got together with the other tenants and said, "We can do better for ourselves and for our children. Why don't we ask the city if we can buy this building and then fix it up? Then we will each *own* our place." It took a lot of work to change people's minds, but she finally accomplished it. They bought their condos, owned them, and had something to be proud of. That place became an example to many other cities.

God wants to lift you to a higher level of leadership. He wants you to grow, advance, multiply, and increase. If your friendships and hangouts are holding you back and producing the wrong attitude in you, have the courage to change them.

3: Reevaluate your current thoughts and attitudes in the light of God's Word

Ask yourself, "Have I been taught wrong?" Sometimes it is hard to recognize if you are operating from your own mind or the mind of Christ. Take a good, hard look at your mental habits, your attitudes, and the fruit you are bearing in your life and area of leadership.

THE "VICTIM" MENTALITY

Some people develop a victim mentality that God hates, but they don't realize it because this attitude is so pervasive in our culture. The victim mentality subtly opposes the promises and goodness of God. It claims that God has no power to change your mind. When you say, "Someone done me wrong; it wasn't fair; because I was wronged I can't move forward," you are basically denying that Jesus has the power to help.

There are many examples in the Bible of the tragic results of unrenewed thinking. Moses sent twelve spies into the Land of Promise, the land that God told the Israelites was meant for their dwelling (see Numbers 13). Ten of them came back and gave a bad report: "Yes, it's a land flowing with milk and honey, but the people are giants—we can never overcome them; they're too big for us!" Two spies believed God's promise. They said: "Yes, the people are big, but our God is bigger. Let's go down and take that land."

The two faith-filled spies went on to live in the Promised Land and greatly prospered. Those with faithless, failure attitudes ended up bleached bones in the desert. This story demonstrates that only a small percentage of those who are saved develop the mind of Christ and a pacesetting attitude. The majority would rather operate from fear and a victim mentality. They believe they are "owed" something because they have been hard done by.

What if Mark, the Gospel writer, said, "There are already a couple of Gospels. Why should I write another one?" What if David had acted like the army of Israel and feared Goliath and his taunting and refused to stand up to him? He was the only one in the whole nation thinking like God. David was fully persuaded that God would give the victory. Look at the results. You must share the mind of Christ and have an attitude that expects victory!

4: Reject old thoughts when they return

In the Navy, we had a room called the Sperry Gyrocompass Room. In that room was the automatic pilot which guided the ship where it had been programmed to go. Not just anyone could enter that room; you had to have security clearance. The function and safety of that gyrocompass was so critical to the success of the ship's mission, that if someone sneaked in and tampered with the coordinates, the ship would end up way off course. We could have ended up in Africa instead of Hawaii.

Your mind and heart are like that gyrocompass. They can be programmed to reach God's destination for your life or some other destination.

The Bible says to guard your heart for it is the wellspring of life. Your heart, the deepest part of your being, guides you through life. Before your mind was renewed, your autopilot was programmed to take you to wrong places. When you came to Christ, when you renewed your mind to be more like Christ's mind, your ability to redirect the autopilot began to grow. It's a constant struggle, but worth it for every pacesetting leader. Let wrong ideas control your mind and you will never arrive at God's destination.

> **Proverbs 4:23 KJV**
> Keep thy heart with all diligence; for out of it are the issues of life.
>
> **Proverbs 4:23 NLT**
> Guard your heart above all else, for it determines the course of your life.

Guard your heart! When you reject thoughts with your conscious mind, they won't be able to enter your unconscious mind. If you do not reject them with your conscious mind, they will go in and become a part of your unconscious motivations. Reject them before they get inside that autopilot room. Remember, your conscious mind can discern and judge but your subconscious mind cannot.

5: Speak words in harmony with God's Word

Your ears love the sound of your voice! When you speak words with your mouth, your mind hears them and gives much more weight to them than anything it hears from someone else. If you repeat a bad report, it goes into your mind and ultimately affects your attitude and actions. If you speak words that do not line up with God's Words, you open the door to failure.

YOU CAN SET YOUR BOUNDARIES

If you're tempted to say, "Oh, I'm just an average leader," why not say instead, "I have the mind of Christ, therefore I am an excellent leader!" You set your own boundaries. Set them as far out as you dare!

God will take you as far as you want to go in harmony with his plan and his Word—the Bible. Speak your new thoughts out loud. The Bible says that with the heart man believes, but with his mouth confession is made. I'm not saying to deny what exists, but when you face reality, speak change to that reality if you need to!

The *truth* (what God thinks) imposed on the current reality will change the current reality to a new reality. When you speak God's solution, you begin the transformation from the inner to the outer. God has a solution for every problem and every situation. As soon as you begin speaking it, your mind and heart are open to receive it.

> **John 6:63 NLT**
> The Spirit alone gives eternal life. Human effort accomplishes nothing. And the very words I have spoken to you are spirit and life.

Jesus' Words have the power to transform! His Words are spirit and life! How does it happen? By repeating the truth time and time again. One repetition adding to another. I have the Bible, or Bible-based messages, going all the time in my car and when I'm at home. I read through the Bible once a year because I need God's Word coming in to keep my thoughts renewed. I have to continually push out old thinking habits, the old furniture of my mind. I need a total, constant renovation. So do you!

If you make excuses, your mind believes those excuses. "I'm too old," you might say. In the Bible, Caleb was eighty-five years old, still strong, and still seizing territory from the enemy.

Or, "I'm too young to be a pacesetting leader." I knew a fifteen-year-old boy named Butch who started a Bible study in Costa Mesa, California. Butch was a member at Calvary Chapel where I attended church. Butch's Bible study grew so big that it outgrew the capacity of the meeting place. So, he went to the Jewish synagogue and rented space from them. Hundreds of people ended up coming to that fifteen-year-old young man's Bible study.

A woman approached Butch one night and said, "Butch, would you pray for my glass eye? It's been bothering me."

Butch said, "That's no problem for God!" He prayed, "Lord, I thank you! You are the Healer. You are the Miracle-Worker. You have resurrection power. Lord, please touch this woman and heal her vision!"

She went home that night and the area behind her glass eye began to itch. She popped it out and saw an eye growing right behind it. It grew into a perfectly normal eye capable of sight!

Butch told his pastor, and the pastor jokingly said, "Butch, how could that happen? You're not even ordained!"

Butch chose to believe God's Word over so-called "reality" and anyone's doubts. God took that faith and used it to work a miracle. Who wouldn't want to experience results like that?

DEVOTIONAL REFLECTIONS

1: **Are there any situations, people, or hangouts that are hindering the renewal of your mind? List them.**

2: Can you identify ideas or attitudes that hold you back from renewing your mind? List a few and then decide how you are going to reject those thoughts when they try to take over your autopilot and get you off God's course for your life.

3: Have you used any excuses for clinging to old habits and ways of thinking? What are they? Now get rid of them!

God wants to lift you to a higher level of leadership. He wants you to grow, advance, multiply, and increase.

Go after everything like you are going to succeed

15

CHAPTER

RENOVATE YOUR MIND: SEE & BELIEVE

Now let us investigate two more vitally important steps in transforming your mind to becoming a pacesetting leader.

6: See and rehearse

Athletes are trained to envision in their minds the game they are about to play. They "see" themselves running their fastest, making the catch, or hitting the ball straight down the fairway. They *see* themselves succeeding.

I learned about this kind of envisioning when I met with Dr. Paul Cho in 1980 in Orchard Park, New York. He related that when he had just thirteen members in his church, he envisioned having a thousand members. That's why he preached with his eyes closed. With his eyes open, he saw thirteen. With his eyes closed, he saw a multitude. Eventually, his church grew to the largest Christian church in the world.

I went home from that meeting and I would practice "seeing" myself as a successful pastor. In my mind, I would rehearse a sermon three or four times. That was how I renewed my thinking and my attitude. Not too many years later I was preaching every week to real people, but it all began with letting the mind of Christ permeate my imagination and renew my thinking.

Some people warned me, "To rehearse things in your mind like that is an occult practice! Don't get into 'envisioning' things." I told them that the devil has a counterfeit for everything, even mental transformation. That doesn't mean we shouldn't renew our minds. There is a movie screen in your mind and if *you* don't put something on it, the devil will. Rehearse the things God puts into your mind as you listen for the thoughts of Christ.

Rehearsing your actions and meditating on your success when it comes to God's will for your life is not an occult practice; it is a powerful tool that God gives you to ensure that you stay the course.

7: Go after everything like you're going to succeed

Nothing of value has ever been accomplished by a person who thought his or her idea was going to fail. Does anyone say, "Well, honey, let's get married. It probably won't work out, but we should at least give it a try for a year." That's the wrong attitude! The right attitude says, "Let's get married for life and have a wonderful time together."

Go into whatever you do expecting 100 percent. When people are sick, pray for them expecting healing. Will you experience success 100 percent of the time? Probably not, because we're still living in this fallen world. But it's okay to believe it is possible and to go for it!

When I invite people to come to Christ, I fully expect people to come to Christ. I do not visualize an empty altar. I fully expect people to be transformed by the Son of God. The world will never be drawn to Jesus, the lost will not seek Jesus, unless his followers radiate a joyous, confident, attitude of hope!

Some psychologists say it takes twenty-one days to change a habit. I want you to act as if nothing you do could possibly fail for the next twenty-one days. Some call it acting; I call it faith. Without Christ we can do *nothing*; through him we can do *everything*.[1]

A friend of mine went to a city of 40,000 people to plant a church. Some said there could never be a successful church plant in that city because of a strong Catholic influence in the area and the high mobility of the population. On average, people moved every three years. My friend said, "I believe that God wants a great church in that city."

The church he planted grew to more than 2,000 members because he would not take into consideration the negative thoughts and faithless attitudes that others tried to use to infect him.

A man in his eighties went to plant a church in Minneapolis, Minnesota. They told him, "It won't work! You can never succeed there." Not only did he do it, he established a mega-church and thousands upon thousands came to Jesus because an eighty-year-old man didn't think he was too old to follow God's will. He renewed his mind and had a positive attitude of success.

Small thinking, poor-attitude leaders will always fail.

When I became pastor of Mount Hope Church, in Lansing, Michigan, local "experts" gave me reasons there would never be a great church in Lansing. The main reason was that another church in town had grown to 700 members, which seemed like a lot then.

Then they told me that there was a "Samson Spirit" in Lansing, so there could never be a great church. (I never did find out what a "Samson Spirit" was!) One seemingly spiritual, old guy told me, "There will never be a great church in Lansing because Lansing is the political seat of the state and there are too many political

---

1 John 15:5; Philippians 4:13

demons here." Another man told me, "We're in the post-Christian era in Lansing."

I rejected all those opinions and believed the Word of God, that says,

Mark 16:17a NLT
These miraculous signs will accompany those who
believe: They will cast out demons in my name....

If there were political devils over Lansing, I thought, we'll cast them out! We're not going to let them stop God's church from growing.

Six years from that time, our church had grown into the thousands. The mayor of the city called me and said, "Pastor Williams, I want somebody that represents God to be the Grand Marshal in the Memorial Day parade. I would also like you to speak at the citywide Memorial Day service. Would you do that?" I joyfully agreed.

Mary Jo, the kids, and I were picked up by this big convertible limousine. Down the street we rode, waving at the people. I looked behind and what did I see? Walking behind our limousine were senators, city council members and other governmental leaders. The Legislature even passed a resolution stating that Pastor Dave Williams was the most influential religious leader in the State of Michigan that year! So much for political demons!

What if I had believed what the naysayers told me? Instead I guarded my autopilot and it took me to a much better place.

SUCCESS STORIES

Some years ago, I knew two men named Doug and Terry who attended a Bible college in Minneapolis. They wanted to work their way through college so they wouldn't graduate with big debt, but there didn't seem to be any available jobs. However, Doug and Terry didn't think like everybody else.

When others dropped out of school and attendance declined, Doug and Terry prayed, "Lord, you called us to this school and we know you will provide a way for us to get through."

One day, they saw an old, dilapidated house for sale. They said, "We could buy that place, fix it up and sell it for a profit!" They got the house for a song, and after school they would paint and make repairs. They put it on the market and it sold for a net profit of $35,000. They bought another one, and another one. Next thing you know, they were hiring students to work for them. When they graduated, Doug and Terry had no college debt and each had $250,000 in cash reserves to get started in ministry! Now, that's pacesetting leadership!

Others say, "I failed in the past. I'm afraid to try again." Consider Babe Ruth; he had more strikeouts than home runs. But what is he remembered for? Home runs!

Isaiah 43:18–19a NKJV
18 "Do not remember the former things, Nor consider the things of old.
19 Behold, I will do a new thing…."

God doesn't consult your past when determining your future.

Some say, "But I got the wrong education." Welcome to the club. I had the wrong education. I was trained in electronics technology and worked for a power company and did electrical work in the Navy. But God said, "I've called you to ministry." My education caught up with my calling as I studied while I worked in ministry.

Philippians 3:12 NKJV
Not that I have already attained, or am already perfected; but I press on, that I may lay hold of that for which Christ Jesus has also laid hold of me.

That is the attitude of a pacesetting leader!

A man named Lee Braxton went to get a job at the bank. Lee had only a sixth-grade education because his father grew sick, and Lee had to drop out of school and stay home to take care of him. The bank wouldn't give him a job, even as a teller, so Lee said, "I'll start my own bank."

His bank became so successful that the people of the community elected him mayor of the city. He subsequently bought a dozen other businesses, became a multimillionaire and retired in his forties so he could help Evangelist Oral Roberts in his ministry. He got Oral Roberts on television back in the 1950s. Lee Braxton didn't have the right education, but he didn't let that stop him.

It doesn't matter who you are or where you are starting. The attitude of a pacesetting leader is constantly renewing, so you are thinking the thoughts of Christ. These steps will help the transformation of your mind and allow your leadership to soar!

IN REVIEW: SEVEN STEPS TO RENEW YOUR MIND

1: You must be born again

2: Accept full responsibility for your mind

3: Reevaluate your current thoughts and attitudes in the light of God's Word

4: Reject old thoughts when they return

5: Speak words in harmony with God's Word

6: See and rehearse

7: Go after everything like you're going to succeed

DEVOTIONAL REFLECTIONS

1: Has anyone ever told you that you would fail at something you felt called to do? What was your response?

2: Who are the positive voices in your life that will build your faith and encourage the renewing of your mind?

3: What possible "excuses" do you have for not becoming a pacesetting leader? Make a quick list.

4: Now cross out each one of those excuses!

5: Take a moment and envision the future you see for yourself by the Holy Spirit. What does it look like?

Vision is looking beyond what you see in the natural.

16

CHAPTER

DEVELOPING THE LEADER'S VISION

Now let us look at one of my favorite subjects: developing the leader's vision. A leader's vision is critical to success. If you can see the invisible, you can accomplish the impossible.

My friend, Tim Redmond, runs the Redmond Leadership Institute. He consults with business leaders and pastors around the nation concerning leadership, growth, and success. One of his foundational principles is that nothing can multiply and grow until a seed is planted. He teaches that if you have an apple seed in your hand, you can see just the apple seed. Or, you can see an apple tree. Or, you can see an entire apple orchard. If your vision is great enough, you can see an apple pie factory. That little seed is filled with powerful potential, if you can see it. If you can see it, you can achieve it. The Bible affirms this principle.

Ephesians 3:20–21 NLT
20 Now all glory to God, who is able, through his mighty power at work within us, to accomplish infinitely more than we might ask or think.

135

²¹ Glory to him in the church and in Christ Jesus
through all generations forever and ever! Amen.

Jesus gave us one of the most powerful Scriptures about vision in this verse.

John 4:35 NKJV
"Do you not say, 'There are still four months and then comes the harvest'? Behold, I say to you, lift up your eyes and look at the fields, for they are already white for harvest!"

SEE THINGS AS THEY SHALL BE

He was teaching his disciples, "Don't see things as they are; see things as they will be!" If you keep seeing things the way they are, if you don't change your vision, you will keep getting the same results. You must see the end result by faith before you can achieve it.

The disciples were ignorant and unlearned men who appeared to lack potential. But Jesus had a vision for those men's futures that others couldn't see. He could see Peter as a mighty apostle preaching on the day of Pentecost, when 3,000 men came to Christ. He could see Matthew and John writing the Gospel accounts. He had ultimate vision.

Some realtors use vision to help you see a wonderful future in a dumpy, rundown house. They paint a word picture: "If you paint this wall here and redesign there, this place would be beautiful!" Realtors like that are the most successful because they give you a vision of what could be rather than what is. Paul wrote about this same subject to the Corinthians.

2 Corinthians 4:18 KJV
While we look not at the things which are seen, but at the things which are not seen: for the things which are seen are temporal; but the things which are not seen are eternal.

If you see things from God's point of view, and begin to speak and act on it, you can accomplish the impossible. True faith sees the invisible becoming real.

What can you see in your life that is invisible? A better marriage? A better business? A greater ministry? A greater income? That vision is eternity working within you to achieve the impossible!

GETTING INTO FOCUS

What would you think of a photographer who started snapping pictures without bothering to focus the camera first? Maybe one photo would turn out, but only by chance. It's much more productive for a photographer to sharply focus on the very best shot and then snap the picture. Likewise, your vision as a pacesetting leader must come into focus.

What does vision mean? We are not talking about a vision as a function of the spiritual gifts, though I believe in supernatural visions and revelations. What I mean by vision is a comprehensive sense of where you are now and where you are going, the big picture of your future. Vision is your heart concept of where you are headed in your ministry, your business, your family, your life.

As I mentioned, when I was 30 years old I began envisioning the future of our church and how it looked. I began praying at the altar at 5:30 in the morning. I would pray, *God, I see this place packed to capacity, and I see ushers setting up chairs.* The sanctuary held 450 people, but our attendance was half that. I envisioned more.

Within a couple of months, I looked out and saw ushers setting up extra chairs because more than 450 people were crowded into the sanctuary. Then I grabbed hold of an even greater vision and prayed, *Lord, I see people filling the balcony!* Now, we didn't even have a balcony, but soon we had to put one in to seat another

100 people. Now 550 people crammed in every Sunday. Next I prayed, *God, I see the choir having to disband so we can seat people in the choir loft!* Sure enough, we had to disband the choir to fit all the people who came into the church. Next, we went to two services, then three services and then five services on Sunday!

The progression happened just as I envisioned it. The interesting thing about seeing the invisible is that when it becomes reality, everybody else is excited, but you have been living in it for years! To me it seemed normal because it was real inside of me before it was real outside of me.

VISION SETS YOU APART

Vision is the motivating force of a church, a business, a life. Vision sets apart real achievers from those who "also ran." Vision is essential to pacesetting leadership. I'm captivated by the realization that fruitfulness, effectiveness, and growth are largely the result of vision, *not* resources. Vision is being able to see the right things, to see what others don't see—to see the apple tree, the apple orchard, and the apple pie factory, all in one little seed.

> **Proverbs 29:18a KJV**
> Where there is no vision, the people perish….

THREE KEYS TO ANY SUCCESSFUL ENDEAVOR

1: **Vision: Seeing the goal and future reality that others don't presently see.**

2: **Knowledge: Getting the know-how, talking to the right people, reading the right books, enlisting the right mentors.**

3: **Obedience: Taking action on the vision. Even though it's invisible you start walking toward it, and you'll see it become reality.**

Next, we will continue to expand our study of a leader's vision.

DEVOTIONAL REFLECTIONS

1: Summarize your vision for a present endeavor whether it's at work, for ministry, or for your personal life.

When you see things that others can't see, even when you are seeing them on the inside, that's what will carry you through those difficult times.

17
CHAPTER

TREADMILL, ELEVATOR, DRIFTER, GUIDED MISSILE

Oral Roberts will probably go down in the history of the Christian church as one of the greatest achievers of all time! He started his healing ministry to take God's power to his generation. Thirty million souls came to Christ during his early ministry, and there is no way of knowing how many others found Jesus as their Savior later on.

Oral Roberts started his great university one day while standing out on a field, praying in the Spirit. God spoke to his heart and said, *Build me a university. Teach the students to know my voice. Teach the students to trust the authority of the Holy Spirit.*

Oral had eleven dollars to his name, but he had a vision. He then surrounded himself with people who knew how to build a university. Next, he took a step of obedience and started sharing that vision with people around the country, until one day out of the ground came Oklahoma's number one tourist attraction: Oral Roberts University.

VISION, NOT RESOURCES, IS THE KEY

It was vision, not resources, that brought it to pass. You may say, "I don't have the money; I don't have the talent; I don't have this; I don't have that...." You only need *one* thing: to see what others don't see. It's called vision—the comprehensive sense of where you are right now and where you are going in the future. Add to that the knowledge and obedience to move from Point A to Point B and you will find the Holy Spirit propels you many steps further. Every time you take a step, the Holy Spirit propels you several extra steps. He always does most of the work.

FOUR TYPES OF PEOPLE

There are four kinds of people as it relates to fruitfulness and effectiveness.

1: Treadmill People

These kind of people work hard, sweat a lot and *seem* to move forward in their lives—but if you analyze their progress they aren't really getting anywhere. They get off the machine the same place they got on. They may be a little healthier, have better leg muscles, but in terms of other progress, there isn't any.

2: Elevator People

This type of person goes up and then down. They appear to have success, but then something happens and back down they go. On average, they end up at the same place they started. For them, every up has a corresponding down.

3: Drifters

These people go wherever the wind blows. Saint Paul spoke about drifters who have not grown in the knowledge of God and in unity of spirit. Drifters are immature and easily led astray by the lies of the devil.

Ephesians 4:14 NLT
Then we will no longer be immature like children.
We won't be tossed and blown about by every wind
of new teaching. We will not be influenced when
people try to trick us with lies so clever they sound
like the truth.

Business people and ministry people should gain knowledge but not drift with every novel new teaching or practice. Things that are blown by the wind never put down roots and produce fruit. Jesus walked with purpose in every step, led by the Spirit.

4: Guided Missiles

This is what you want to be. These people have direction, purpose, mission, and a strong vision! They are authentic leaders who can see the invisible and accomplish the impossible.

If a leader falls into one of the first three categories, look out! Lack of vision always ends in tragedy.

1 Samuel 3:1 NKJV
Now the boy Samuel ministered to the Lord before
Eli. And the word of the Lord was rare in those days;
there was no widespread revelation.

This verse tells of a time when there was no shared vision in Israel. People did what they believed to be right in their own eyes. It was a time of chaos and everyone lost. If a nation, or a person, does not have a big, inspiring view of the future, that nation, or that person, is not going anywhere.

A few years ago, I spoke at Phoenix First Assembly for Pastor Tommy Barnett. I publicly complemented Pastor Barnett, saying how I love how he dreams big dreams. After the service, a man came up to me and said, "You mentioned our pastor's dreams. There's only one problem. We can't afford all his dreams!" I thought, *I hope this guy isn't in leadership here!*

143

People with no vision will criticize those who do have vision. They will say, "You have no resources for that. How are you going to do it?" For them it's never the right time to take action on a vision. They even try to hinder the process when you begin. They nitpick everything. The Pharisees had no vision of God's future and so they were enemies of Jesus. They wanted business as usual. They had Jesus executed to maintain their status quo.

Florence Chadwick was an endurance swimmer back in the 1950s. She was the first woman to ever swim the English Channel in both directions, from England to France, and France to England. In 1952, she attempted to swim from Catalina Island in the Pacific Ocean to the shore of California—a trip of 26 miles. As she swam, boats surrounded her and people watched for sharks, everyone wanted to witness this historic event.

Suddenly, a fog rolled in and she could no longer see the shoreline. She stopped a half a mile short of her destination because she didn't know how much farther she had to go.

Two months later she tried again. Again a fog set in, but she kept going until she walked onto the shore of California. They asked her how she did it. She said, "This time I kept a vision in my mind of the shoreline. I didn't know exactly where it was, but when the fog set in, I kept seeing the shoreline in my mind."

This demonstrates an amazing principle: When you see things that others can't see, even when you are seeing them on the inside, it can carry you through those difficult times, those times when you're in the wilderness, those times when you are facing trials.

One of the top reasons businesses go bankrupt and ministries fail is lack of vision, the intangible quality that is perhaps the most important factor in success in any area of life.

Next we will highlight some of the vision blockers you will encounter on the path to pacesetting leadership.

DEVOTIONAL REFLECTIONS

1: **What kind of person are you?**
   - **Treadmill**
   - **Elevator**
   - **Drifter**
   - **Guided missile**

2: **What factors caused you to make that choice?**

3: **Have you ever stopped short of a goal because you ran out of vision?**

4: **Next time, what will keep you going?**

Beware of things that will freeze the fuel line of vision.

18

VISION BLOCKERS

What hinders vision? There are several areas in which you can potentially experience difficulties; here are seven of the worst vision blockers I have noted at work in lives, businesses, and ministries.

1: Failing to reach beyond yourself

Any business or church can become a smug, self-centered club. When you stop looking beyond yourself, you will become self-centered and stop serving others. Your vision dims. You forget that God called you to minister to someone else's needs. Instead, you get distracted by striving to meet your own needs. That immediately limits your vision.

Vision is for others too, not just yourself! Don't let a self-centered tendency block your success as a leader.

2: Aiming for "just" average

The average church has fewer than 100 people, so should the pastor of a 200 member church feel successful? Of course not! But when you set the standard based on the average, your aim will be too low.

Don't set your vision by the average achievements you see around you. Don't get satisfied when you do just a *little* better. Aim much higher than average!

3: Taking unity lightly

In a family, church, or business a house divided cannot stand.

Mark 3:25 KJV
And if a house be divided against itself, that house cannot stand.

In my early years as a pastor, a certain man would speak publicly against some of my policies. He didn't agree with them, so he would actually prophesy in the name of the Lord to convince people that my policies were wrong.

More than one vision equals "di"-vision. My vision wasn't his vision; we were not in unity. He soon left the church.

Another man said, "I don't like all this talk about growth. I think we should keep the membership to 250 people so we can know everybody."

I said, "Brother, that is not my vision, and there are not going to be two visions in this church. Make a decision. Come under the framework of the pastor's vision, or go somewhere where your vision will fit."

Someone else had a vision of a family-run church, telling me, "This is a family-run church, and we hire the pastor as sort of a Sunday chaplain. He does everything we want him to do."

"That's not the vision God gave me." I responded. "I want to be a New Testament pastor, equipping saints for the work of the ministry. So you have a choice. Come under the framework of the vision of the pastor or go somewhere else."

One fellow wanted us to become a demon-expert church. He wanted to gather groups to go picket cults. I said, "That is not included in the framework of my vision. I would rather shine a light in a dark place than go out and bellyache about the dark."

It's the same way in business. If you have an employee who doesn't share your vision of the business, you have to cut him or her loose. Multiple visions is division! Division is not God's mathematics. Paul said to avoid those who cause divisions.

Romans 16:17 AMP
I appeal to you, brethren, to be on your guard concerning those who create dissensions and difficulties and cause divisions, in opposition to the doctrine (the teaching) which you have been taught. [I warn you to turn aside from them, to] avoid them.

Mary Jo and I have found that when we agree together on something, it comes to pass, even if one of us has to say, "Okay, I'll back off here. Let it be according to your will, and I'll agree with you." Every time we've gotten in total agreement and supported the same vision, it has come to pass.

4: Tolerating evil actions and words

2 Corinthians 12:20–21 MSG
I do admit that I have fears that when I come you'll disappoint me and I'll disappoint you, and in frustration with each other everything will fall to pieces—quarrels, jealousy, flaring tempers, taking sides, angry words, vicious rumors, swelled heads, and general bedlam. I don't look forward to a second humiliation by God among you, compounded by hot tears over that crowd that keeps sinning over and over in the same old ways, who refuse to turn away from the pigsty of evil, sexual disorder, and indecency in which they wallow.

These kinds of obviously evil activities will block a leader's vision from coming to pass and cause a general disintegration.

5: Putting a dollar sign on everything

When a business or ministry becomes overly obsessed with immediate profit or revenue, the vision shrinks. Years ago, our church acquired a bus. Instead of painting nice letters on the side of the bus that said "Mount Hope Church," one trustee wanted to do it with electrician's tape to save the church some money. He had a vision of the church being too poor to afford decent lettering! It might seem that he was trying to save money, but in truth his mind was more on money and his perceived lack than on God's infinite ability to provide.

I knew a man who owned a restaurant with good food but little business. His place looked crummy. Weeds grew up through the concrete in the parking lot, which wasn't even marked with spaces. He had no drive-thru, even though he sold fast food. I asked, "Why don't you spruce up your property a little bit?"

He replied, "It costs too much money!" He ended up selling the business to a man who cleaned up the parking lot, painted in parking spots, and built in a drive-thru window. Now at lunch time that place is humming with business. It's all about making an investment. The previous owner thought he couldn't afford to fix up his restaurant. In truth, he couldn't afford not to.

It's easy to tell if someone puts a dollar sign on everything: you will hear him or her say, "Well, in this economy...." That's how you know they have no vision. God has great plans for those who see the invisible. They will accomplish the impossible. Those who look only at the money, or the present economy, will only get what their measly dollars or the what their "economy" can provide.

6: Being passive and satisfied with mediocrity and lack of excellence

Quality attracts quality. Mediocrity attracts mediocrity. Do you have persistent trouble in a department of your business or church? Check the leadership to see what they are attracting.

7: Becoming bored with your job or ministry

Serving God in ministry, business, or family is the most exciting thing on earth! If you ever become bored, then somehow your vision for the future has been lost. It's time to stop and re-focus.

CALL AND WAIT

How do you get vision? By calling on God. A vision must be sought, seen, and shared. It does not usually drop on you from the sky.

Jeremiah 33:3 NKJV
"Call to Me, and I will answer you, and show you great and mighty things, which you do not know."

God will give you vision if you ask him. Notice he didn't say, "I'm going to *tell* you great and mighty things," but, "I'm going to *show* you great and mighty things. Things you don't know and couldn't find out any other way."

He will show you how to solve a perplexing business problem, or a difficult issue in the church, or a troubling situation in your family. He will give you a picture of what it will be like when the solution is applied. That is vision, and it comes directly from God.

When I was invited to be the pastor of Mount Hope Church, I was nothing more than a young, inexperienced "green bean." I had never been the pastor of a church before and I had no idea how to do it. Some leaders swing into action and start doing all the things that everyone else does. That has a certain logical appeal, but I wanted more. I wanted God's vision, not just my puny little efforts.

So early each morning I waited before the Lord at the altar when no one was there except God and me. God began to show me things. Acts 13:44 popped off the page...

Acts 13:44 KJV
And the next sabbath day came almost the whole city together to hear the word of God.

God gave me the vision that it was possible for the entire city to become disciples of Jesus. I saw the people getting up every week and coming to church.

Later I was talking to a man who was new to our church. I asked him how he found us. He said, "I was transferred here for work, and when I got to town I went to the Bible bookstore. I asked what was a good local church and the clerk said, 'You might as well go to Mount Hope Church—everybody else in town does!'" God gave that vision and even others began to believe it.

CREATIVE LOAFING

I also do something you might think unusual. I call it "creative loafing." I was inspired to this practice by this verse...

Isaiah 40:31 NKJV
But those who wait on the Lord Shall renew their strength; They shall mount up with wings like eagles, They shall run and not be weary, They shall walk and not faint.

It doesn't help your vision to put your hand to the plow and never take time to rest and enjoy God. So I try to get "loafy" sometimes. Some of the greatest ideas have come to me when I got quiet before the Lord and said, "I can't untangle this mess. I can't put this vision together, I don't know how to do it." I wait on God in an easy, relaxed way.

I encourage you as a pacesetting leader to occasionally "loaf" around with the Lord. Say, "I'm going to take an hour or two and just wait before God." Forget the work, the email, the text messages, and voice mails. Get alone with God. Get his vision burned in you, and step-by-step you'll accomplish what others said was impossible.

When you exercise the discipline of calling and waiting on God, hope and renewed vision will come. You will receive a vision from heaven and it will fuel your efforts. You will see the invisible; you will accomplish the impossible.

Every painting starts out invisible. Every masterpiece began as a blank canvas and an idea. One brush stroke at a time the vision emerged. But it started with what others couldn't see. God has a vision for you. Do you see it?

DEVOTIONAL REFLECTIONS

1: **Which of the seven vision blockers most apply to your present situation? Explain why.**

2: **What steps will you take to deal with the vision blockers most troubling you right now?**

3: **Do you need to take some time for loafing with the Lord? Set time this week to spend time in his presence doing nothing but waiting and relaxing.**

Note: I would love to have you attend a **Faith Goals Retreat.** *This two-day retreat is designed for pastors, business leaders, entrepreneurs, and high achievers. It is a relaxed time of learning about vision and how to take a vision and "micro-step" it to fulfillment. Contact Dave Williams Ministries at 517-731-0000, or visit www.davewilliams.com/itinerary for more information about future* **Faith Goals Retreats.**

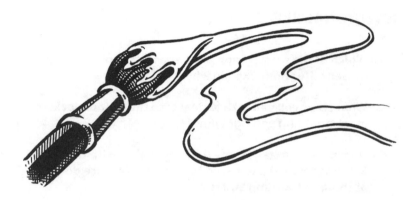

Faith goals are like brush strokes in the masterpiece

19

FAITH GOALS

Yogi Berra said, "If you don't know where you are going, you might wind up someplace else."

As a leader, success depends on your ability to take your vision—your macro-picture—and convert it into reality through a series of micro-steps. Converting vision into reality is the process of setting and reaching faith goals. When I learned this, it transformed my life.

God will not do his work on earth by himself—he insists on working with you.

Mark 16:20 NKJV
And they went out and preached everywhere, the Lord working with them and confirming the word through the accompanying signs. Amen.

God always works this way. Jesus' birth is a perfect example: He was born of the Virgin Mary and conceived of the Holy Spirit—a partnership between God and a woman. God wants to work with you in close partnership to bring your vision to reality.

Years ago, psychologists discovered that 95 percent of people have no written goals, and thus they fall into what they called the "underachiever" category. The other 5 percent have written goals and succeed more often than the 95 percent combined. Understanding vision and faith goals tells me why that is so. It is because the power of specific goals moves you toward your bigger vision.

Jim Rohn, the late business philosopher once said, "I find it fascinating that most people plan their vacations with better care than they plan their lives. Perhaps it's because escape is easier than change."

Faith goals help you get directly from Point A to Point B instead of wandering in circles. When I was twelve years old, the park near our house had a piece of play equipment we called a "maypole." Hanging from the top of the pole were six chains, each with a triangular handle. My buddies and I would go over there, grab those handles and start running around the maypole. When we had enough momentum, we would lift our feet off the ground and fly around until it slowed down again. But as fun as it was, we always ended up in the same place.

Many people are like that in life. They work, spinning their wheels, but not getting anywhere. Their problem is not spiritual or attitudinal but practical. They are not setting and meeting faith goals. The Beatles had a song called *Nowhere Man*.[1]

He's a real nowhere Man,
Sitting in his Nowhere Land,
Making all his nowhere plans,
For nobody.
Doesn't have point of view,
Knows not where he's going to,
Isn't he a bit like you and me?

---

[1] Lennon, John; McCarney, Paul; *Nowhere Man*, © Sony/ATV Music Publishing LLC, Universal Music Publishing Group.

I hope this man is *not* a bit like you. A nowhere man going no place, with no goals and no targets. Without faith goals, vision eventually dies and you become a nowhere man or woman.

Who would buy a ticket for a cruise that didn't post a destination? Who would take a boat that promised to drift wherever the tide took it? What if the captain welcomed everybody aboard and said, "My vision is to have a great trip, but I don't know how to pull it off. We'll just have to see where we end up." You can almost hear the stampede of people exiting the boat!

BRUSH STROKES OF VISION

Once you have the vision for your life, your business, your church, or your ministry it's time to turn the macro-picture into micro-steps that propel you toward the vision's fulfillment. Faith goals are brush strokes in the broader masterpiece. There is great power in micro-stepping toward your macro-picture. Faith goals put feet to your vision. Without faith goals, your vision is just a dream.

In 52 days, Nehemiah accomplished what people said couldn't be accomplished in years. With the power of faith goals, he led the people to build a wall around Jerusalem. Yet most people are like the man who stood on the side of the road randomly shooting into the woods and called himself a hunter. You're only a hunter if you're aiming at something! You only have vision if you are moving in faith toward a goal.

> **1 Corinthians 9:26 NLT**
> So I run with purpose in every step. I am not just shadowboxing.

> **1 Corinthians 9:26 AMP**
> Therefore I do not run uncertainly (without definite aim). I do not box like one beating the air and striking without an adversary.

In other words, you don't just flail around without an idea of what you want to accomplish. You move with purpose to fulfill a concrete goal. You do not just expend energy for no reason.

Mark 9:23 NLT
"What do you mean, 'If I can'?" Jesus asked. "Anything is possible if a person believes."

Mark 11:24 NKJV
Therefore I say to you, whatever things you ask when you pray, believe that you receive them, and you will have them.

The words "anything" and "things" in these passages mean goals or objects. Faith is the substance of "things" (goals, objectives, targets) that you hope for. Jesus wants you to set faith goals!

Your vision can be big and general, but a goal should be small and actionable. For example, "I want to be healthy" is not a goal, it's a vision. A faith goal might be, "I will spend 25 minutes a day on a treadmill or stationary bike." Yet most people's goals are so general that they lead to no specific action.

Faith can only go after specific things. Faith is the substance of "things" hoped for—meaning specific, concrete things. Your faith cannot be activated without specifics.

When I was a boy we had magnifying glasses at school. On a sunny day, we could set leaves on fire by focusing the sun through the magnifying glass like a little laser. That is the same way faith goals work, like a magnifying glass focusing our efforts on one thing at a time. Faith goals give focus to faith. Faith has to be focused like a magnifying glass on one thing.

Our church sent a team to build a church in Costa Rica. That was the vision, and so we had to micro-step it out. We screened the people who wanted to go. We got airline tickets, arranged ground transportation, got all the lumber and bricks on site and, in less than two weeks, we had a brand new church built in Costa Rica. Everybody knew the part they had to play. A hundred little brush strokes—faith goals—went into creating a masterpiece.

I heard someone say, "Faith goals are dangerous. They can hurt your self-image because if you don't reach them, you will be disappointed in yourself." I see it much differently.

Having faith goals brings you much closer to your vision than you would be without them. If you're a student and you aim for an "A" and earn a "B", isn't that better than if you had set no goal and got a "C" or "D"? When I pray for someone's healing, I believe 100 percent of the time that he or she will be healed. Is everyone that I minister to healed? No. But through setting faith goals, I see more people healed than ministers who won't even try to minister to the sick.

Nehemiah 9:28a KJV
But after they had rest, they did evil again before thee: therefore leftest thou them in the land of their enemies, so that they had the dominion over them....

Without faith goals, life is aimless. Nehemiah 9:28 tells the story of the children of Israel. They rested too long and "did evil." They accomplished one faith goal but didn't set the next one, so what did they do? They did evil. Why do people follow evil? Because they don't have faith goals to follow.

Faith goals take you closer to fulfilling that wonderful vision you have for your life—that invisible thing that God wants for you. Next we'll study some practical rules for goal-setting that will help you for the rest of your life.

DEVOTIONAL REFLECTIONS

1: What are your specific faith goals? Jot them down.

2: Name some of the faith goals you have already set and met?

3: Ask God to inspire your mind with specific goals that will take you toward your vision.

*Editor's Note: Far a more in depth study on faith goals, please Dr. Dave Williams' book, **The Miracle of Faith Goals** available online at www.decapolispublishing.com. This title is also available on Nook, Kindle, and ibooks.*

Once you have the vision...it's time to
turn the macro-picture
into micro-steps....

Ruthlessly reject opportunities that point away from your vision.
Focus on the goal!

20

SIX RULES FOR GOAL SETTING

These rules for goal-setting can be absolutely transformational for you and your leadership.

1: Faith goals are always specific and concrete

"My goal is just to be used of God," you emote, but that is not specific. What does that statement mean in a concrete, practical way? What would you have to do, learn, or become in order for God to use you? It's almost impossible to go after an ethereal, formless idea or concept. In what specific way do you want to be used of God? What steps do you intend to take?

If your God-given vision is to become a preacher, then you should set some specific faith goals. Goals to read books by successful ministers, undertake an intensive Bible study, take classes on preaching and public speaking, talk to a preacher about the traits you should be developing in your life and personality, and then set goals that will enable you to go to school to earn credentials to become a pastor.

If you want to be a business owner, your faith goals should be to find a mentor who can help you, read business books, and perhaps enroll in a business college.

If your vision is to get married, one faith goal might be to make a list of who you would consider marrying, or the qualities and characteristics you want in a spouse. Or a list of the qualities and personality traits you would need to develop in yourself that would attract a spouse to you. For instance, improve my table manners, dress attractively, have my teeth whitened, etc.

2: Prayerfully set your own goals

Don't let somebody else set your goals for you. Unless the goals are your own, your heart will not be in them. When you set your own faith goals, your enthusiasm is sustained. The goals burn within you. You won't need someone else to keep encouraging you. Like David in the Bible, you learn how to encourage yourself. Your faith goals should be specific and personal to your vision.

3: A faith goal should always move you closer to fulfilling your vision

Once I heard a man say, "I am called to the ministry, but I'm working at General Motors and they're providing free education for those who want to study chemistry. So I'll take the chemistry classes because they're free."

The chemistry class may be free, but how is it taking you closer to your vision? My advice: Ruthlessly reject opportunities that point away from your vision. Otherwise you may spend your life on activities that move you away from the call God has placed on your life.

Goals help you organize your life. When you have vision and faith goals, life is a lot less work because you have a way of screening everything. You simply ask yourself when an opportunity comes along, "Does this idea or opportunity fit within my vision? Does it match up with my faith goals?" If not, you can confidently say, "No, I'm sorry, that's not part of the plan." This explains why New Year's resolutions never work.

A goal casually set and lightly taken will be freely abandoned at the first obstacle.   ~Zig Ziglar

Every opportunity you take should somehow bring you closer to fulfilling your vision.

4: A faith goal should be written down

Some people keep everything in their heads, but I have found that the palest ink is stronger than the sharpest memory. Get it down on paper. When you do, you'll achieve a hundred times more in your lifetime.

1 Chronicles 28:19 NLT
"Every part of this plan," David told Solomon, "was given to me in writing from the hand of the Lord."

The Lord guided David as he set faith goals and put them in writing. He wrote, "*Every* part of this plan...." meaning the plan was detailed. I love that!

Don't give yourself a chance to forget your faith goals. Write them down and keep them in a prominent place to remind yourself of where you are going next. I have a notebook called "Dave's Faith Goals." There is a picture of me on the front. Inside are pictures I've taken from the internet and cut out of magazines that illustrate my vision as a leader. I track the progress of my faith goals and am encouraged when they are accomplished. I encourage you to get a notebook like that for writing down your faith goals and see how it will transform your life.

5: A faith goal must be challenging

Mark 16:15 KJV
And he said unto them, Go ye into all the world, and preach the gospel to every creature.

Jesus did not tell his disciples, "I'll be satisfied with 200 followers. Go into all the world and when you've got 200 more disciples, that should be enough." No, he gave a challenging vision that seemed impossible—except that God was in it.

Our faith goals should challenge and stimulate us like that. Don't be wimpy when setting a faith goal. Make it interesting and challenging enough to keep your attention and motivation going. Don't make it impossible, like creating a new planet, but do make it something that will draw out your best talents, planning, perseverance, and creativity.

6: A faith goal has to have a deadline

If you got engaged to someone but never set a wedding date, chances are you would never get married. You would drift from month-to-month, year-to-year waiting for the right moment to strike. Faith goals always have deadlines. A great Bible example is the story of the woman with the issue of blood. She came to Jesus with a vision and faith goals—including a deadline. She said, "If I just touch the hem of his robe, I know I will be healed." So she pressed in through the crowd and touched his robe. She got her miracle.

> **Luke 8:43–48 MSG**
> [43-45] In the crowd that day there was a woman who for twelve years had been afflicted with hemorrhages. She had spent every penny she had on doctors but not one had been able to help her. She slipped in from behind and touched the edge of Jesus' robe. At that very moment her hemorrhaging stopped. Jesus said, "Who touched me?" When no one stepped forward, Peter said, "But Master, we've got crowds of people on our hands. Dozens have touched you."
> [46] Jesus insisted, "Someone touched me. I felt power discharging from me."
> [47] When the woman realized that she couldn't remain hidden, she knelt trembling before him. In

front of all the people, she blurted out her story—
why she touched him and how at that same moment she was healed.
[48] Jesus said, "Daughter, you took a risk trusting
me, and now you're healed and whole. Live well,
live blessed!"

God modeled this process for us, too. He had a wonderful
vision of redemption for mankind. He knew that man was
going to sin, and so God's plan to restore us proceeded from
one deadline to another. Step-by-step, he made faith announce-
ments down the centuries through people we call prophets. He
told them, "The Messiah is coming. He's going to be born in
Bethlehem. He's going to be crucified and raised from the dead.
He's going to ascend to heaven and the Church will begin and
grow in this period of time." God set faith goals and deadlines
for his plan of redemption. He does this for everything. The
apostle Paul wrote,

Romans 5:6 NLT
When we were utterly helpless, Christ came at just
the right time and died for us sinners.

Notice the phrase "at just the right time." God knew all along
when Jesus would be born, when he would die, when he would
rise again. He has a time for everything!

God works by goals. He has faith goals for your life and a
faith goal for the day and the hour when Jesus comes back. We
should have deadlines with our goals, too. Remember that work
expands to fill the time allotted. That is called Parkinson's Law.
So make deadlines that are not too soon and not too far away.
Try to fit the deadline to the goal.

Faith goals will change you on the inside. They will shape the
way you think. Ultimately, setting faith goals is not about what
you get but about what you become. Let's commit as leaders to

have a great, big, God-given vision for our lives and then to set and reach faith goals for our leadership at home, in ministry, and in the workplace.

DEVOTIONAL REFLECTIONS

1: Do you have any faith goals you are pursuing right now? What are they?

2: Ask the Lord, what faith goals you should be pursuing? Pray about this in the coming days and then write down specifically what you will do.

3: This week, buy a faith goal journal or establish a place to write down your faith goals.

God works by goals.

Constant stress becomes distress and is harmful to your leadership, your mind, and your body.

21

DISTRESS SIGNALS
IN LEADERSHIP

This chapter could literally save your life. And because of the seriousness of this topic I want to start with some funny headlines to relieve any stress you might feel as we begin! These quotes are taken from actual newspapers articles:

- County to Pay $250,000 to Advertise Lack of Funds
- Volunteers Search for Old Civil War Planes
- Army Vehicle Disappears—Australian army vehicle worth $74,000 has gone missing after being painted with camouflage.
- Caskets Found as Workers Demolish Mausoleum
- Ten Commandments: Supreme Court Says Some Okay, Some Not
- Alton Attorney Accidentally Sues Himself
- Federal Agents Raid Gun Shop, Find Weapons
- Statistics Show Teen Pregnancy Drops Off Significantly After Age 25
- One-Armed Man Applauds the Kindness of Strangers

- Prisoner Serving 2,000 Year Sentence Could Face More Time

I hope these made you laugh, and I hope you got the point as well—as a leader you will have to find relief from some of the pressures that will come your way.

Life can be stressful for a leader because everyone wants a piece of you. It's easy to feel like you're always failing to meet expectations, falling behind, and pulled in multiple directions. Your calendar gets full, challenges get big, and you find yourself stuck in the trenches day after day, not rising high enough to see the big picture. Laughter goes away because the pressures and demands seem so great. If you are a leader in any capacity, you have faced this kind of distress already.

SOME STRESS IS IMPORTANT

Some stress is good. It stimulates you and keeps you interested in what you are doing. If you play guitar, you know those strings have to be tightened to a certain level to be in tune. The same with a piano or a violin. The strings have to be stressed to just the perfect level to make beautiful music. You need stress, but there is a perfect tension of stress. Too little and you are bored. Too much and you are distressed. When you are bored, you are under-stressed, and when you are overstressed, you are distressed. Neither condition is good.

Constant stress becomes distress and is harmful to your leadership, your mind, and your body. Prolonged distress can cause hyper-coagulation of the blood, creating heart attacks or strokes. Too much stress can lead to high blood pressure, irritability, depression, and feelings of failure. There are a hundred ways that distress harms us physically and mentally.

Distress reminds me of an incident that happened some years ago when an airplane nearly crashed. An island-hopper flight in

Hawaii was cruising along when the crew began hearing strange noises. Suddenly the top of the airplane blew away and a flight attendant was sucked from the plane to her death. Everyone wearing a seat belt was okay, and the pilot was able to land the plane despite the big hole in its top. The authorities determined the cause of failure was "metal stress." When airplanes take off and land they pressurize and depressurize. There is a constant expansion and contraction of the metal that compromises the strength of the metal over time, especially in "puddle-jumper" flights that frequently take off and land.

ALL LEADERS FACE STRESS

In leadership you find the same kinds of stress acting on your mind and body. It has been said that all of us are in one of three stages: going into a trial, in a trial, or just coming out of a trial. My personal experience has proven this is true!

How do you handle stress in leadership? First, it's helpful to remember that all leaders face stress. At some point almost every leader tries to do too much for too long with too little. Moses tried to manage every detail of leading the Israelites. He became so stressed he actually wanted to die, until God gave him the solution to his distress. If you're loving Jesus and growing as a leader, you can be sure there will be pressures.

King David faced high stress that turned into distress. Listen to his mood in this Psalm.

> **Psalm 25:15 KJV**
> Mine eyes are ever toward the Lord; For he shall pluck my feet out of the net.

When facing distress you feel trapped in a net. You want to escape, but you can't. You need some time for yourself but can't take a vacation. You feel trapped.

Once I was facing a number of stressful situations, and I remember saying, "It feels like I have a pegboard with twelve holes and thirty pegs all wanting in. The pegs I don't have room for are screaming for me to make room, so I take one out and put a different one in, and then the first one starts screaming." It was an incredibly stressful time for me. David was incredibly stressed and cried out to God.

Psalm 25:16–20 KJV
[16] Turn thee unto me, and have mercy upon me; for I am desolate and afflicted.
[17] The troubles of my heart are enlarged: O bring thou me out of my distresses.
[18] Look upon mine affliction and my pain; and forgive all my sins.
[19] Consider mine enemies; for they are many; and they hate me with cruel hatred.
[20] O keep my soul, and deliver me: let me not be ashamed; for I put my trust in thee.

I am sure you have offered up a similar cry at some point in life, "God, bring me out of my distresses!" The apostle Paul faced severe stress and described it this way.

2 Corinthians 1:8 NKJV
For we do not want you to be ignorant, brethren, of our trouble which came to us in Asia: that we were burdened beyond measure, above strength, so that we despaired even of life.

Paul's pressures were so great that he thought he was going to die. Have you faced anything like that before?

You can't always tell by looking at someone if he or she has moved beyond stress into distress. People tend to hide their strong emotions and may seem happy-go-lucky even though they are in turmoil. The same may be true of you.

Leaders, by nature, want to keep going and not acknowledge their systems are failing. For that reason it isn't always obvious, even to yourself, that you have moved into distress. Here are some warning signs of distress to carefully watch for in your life.

1: Forgetfulness

"Where did I put my keys?" "Where are my glasses?" "Oh, I forgot about that appointment!" When you start forgetting basic things, or even people's names that you've known for twenty years, your mind may be distressed.

2: Trouble seeing alternative solutions

When you are distressed you think there is only one way of dealing with a challenge. You get frustrated when something blocks that path.

3: Temper flare-ups

Sometimes you just "blow your top." You don't mean to, but you're under a lot of pressure. Sometimes you may even surprise yourself by your lack of self control.

4: Inability to change harmful patterns

Instead of controlling your thoughts and behaviors, your thoughts and behaviors begin to control you. You may sleep too little or too much and not be able to control it. You may find it difficult to push away negative, condemning thoughts. You might think God is upset with you. You might dwell on everything you've ever done wrong. You might think repeatedly, "I am a total failure." Instead of acknowledging a little failure here or there, you magnify every flaw, fault, or failure to an extreme. Every little thing that happens appears to reinforce your negative ideas.

5: You lose sight of any reward

It seems like no matter what you do or how well you do it, the reward won't be worth it anyway.

6: Feelings of helplessness

You are caught in a net and feel absolutely helpless to do anything. You call on God, but it seems like he doesn't answer.

7: Finally you become cynical and negative

After too long a period of unrelieved stress you become mentally, emotionally, and physically exhausted. You say, "Nothing good happens to me. Good things happen to others—they deserve them. But good things never happen to me—I don't deserve a break."

Your body and mind can only take so much stress before failing. Like the airplane that flew too long without proper maintenance of its metal frame and failed, you must find relief from stress, or you will fail.

In the next chapter we'll examine ways of overcoming and avoiding distress.

DEVOTIONAL REFLECTIONS

1: Are you in distress right now? Which of the above signs tell you so?

2: Have you felt trapped or overly frustrated lately? Why?

3: Who knows you well enough to tell you that you seem to be distressed?

Constant stress becomes distress and is harmful to your leadership, your mind, and your body.

The best way to handle stress is to go directly to God

22

HOW TO HANDLE STRESS

A 35 year old man worked at a department store; he was in charge of snow removal. But people would leave their cars in the parking lot overnight, so he couldn't remove the snow completely. So, his boss would scream at him. One day, he didn't come home. His wife was worried, so they checked his office and found him sitting at his desk—dead. The pressure had gotten so great and he didn't know how to handle it in a healthy way. His body literally gave up. The same thing often happens to elderly people when one spouse dies, the surviving partner is not far behind because death created so much distress.

WRONG RESPONSES TO DISTRESS

How do you, as a pacesetting leader, successfully respond to distress? There are some wrong ways.

One wrong way is when you come against a problem you say, "I can do all things through Christ who strengthens me!" Then you heedlessly, relying on your own strength, charge at your

179

problem like a bull, banging your head into whatever gets in your way. You refuse to accept the fact that distress might derail you. That's not smart and it's not realistic.

Or, you could simply withdraw from stressful situations. Refusing to face problems is why people drift from organization to organization, job to job, church to church, and marriage to marriage. They come against a problem and run away!

Maybe you like to direct your anger toward those around you. You blame others and find fault Refusing to take responsibility is only going to add to your distress.

Another dysfunctional way to handle stress is self blame. You point the finger of blame at yourself and feel like a failure. That leads to depression and loss of focus.

Sometimes God, in his perfect wisdom, allows walls for a reason—perhaps to grow you up or slow you down. For example, when our church was building a large, new facility, we ran out of money after the foundation was poured. I put a stop to the project because I refused to borrow money from the bank. I felt God wanted us to build it debt-free, but I couldn't seem to raise enough money to finish the project. Weeds grew up on the property. There stood the sign—"Future Home of Mount Hope Church." People told me, "You're the laughing stock of the community. You started something and couldn't finish it." At times I felt they were right.

Then one day I got a call from a Senator who offered to help us re-start the project without borrowing money from the bank. In preparing for construction, the contractors came out to the property and ran tests on the foundation that was already poured. They discovered that the wrong concrete had been used. If we had built on that foundation, the building might have collapsed on the day we opened.

God put a wall in front of us for a reason! As soon as we dealt with the faulty concrete, the money rolled in. We had $2 million in cash in six months to start the project. We built the $6.2 million dollar worship center in 1987 without ever going to the bank for a loan! The distress I had felt was because God was getting my attention about a major problem.

KEY CAUSES OF DISTRESS

When you recognize the causes of distress, you can minimize and avoid them more effectively. Here are a few key causes you should try to minimize or avoid.

1: Distress: Interruptions

When I was a young pastor, I had an office with glass windows. Everybody knew when I was in the office, and I found that people dropped in just to drink coffee and tell me what they bought at the mall. I needed to be working, but I was constantly subjected to interruptions.

Once a man came in and sat down. He began to talk; he was hard of hearing so it was difficult to converse with him. I mostly listened. He told amazing stories, and it was really interesting, but three hours of my time were gone just like that. The next day he came back again for another three hours. I kept thinking, *I've got a hundred other things I should be doing, and here I am listening to the same stories I heard yesterday.*

The next day, a car pulled into the parking lot. I looked out the window and there he was. I dove under my desk and hid there. I could hear him asking, "Is Pastor Dave in?"

My secretary said, "Well, he was in there. I don't know where he went! Maybe he just went to the rest room."

The man replied, "I'll just sit here and wait for him."

I was hiding under that desk for at least half an hour praying, "Jesus, deliver me!" When he finally left, I came out feeling guilty that I had hidden. At the same time I learned a valuable lesson. If you don't control your time, someone else will. Interruptions create a lot of stress.

After that I put a door to the outside in my office, so when I saw one of these professional time-taker-uppers coming, I could slip out the back door and my secretary wouldn't be lying by saying, "He's not in his office." It worked great!

As a pacesetting leader, you must do your best to insulate yourself from interruptions. Some interruptions are important, but most are not. Don't feel guilty when you insulate yourself. You will know the ones who are God's interruptions. Listen to those but avoid the rest. That may mean screening your calls or hiring a secretary. Free yourself from the tyranny of having to answer every call that comes in or respond to every email. It will save you a lot of distress.

2: Distress: Meetings

Ineffective meetings that go too long and have no clear objectives cause stress. I finally said to the Lord, "I will serve on no more boards unless I know what time the meeting starts and when it ends." Beware of serving on boards that have no real purpose and are inconsiderate of your time.

3: Distress: Disorganization and lack of planning

I keep a journal with me at all times and jot down ideas, plans, organizational structure, and priorities. When I am organized I am less overwhelmed by the number of things I have to do. Sometimes you can feel so overwhelmed that you actually don't start anything. You look around at the heap of items to do, and you become paralyzed. The solution is to ignore the size of the stack and plunge in somewhere specific. Don't fixate on the number of items—tackle one thing at a time. You will get through things a lot faster than you thought you could.

4: Distress: Trying to do too much

This kind of distress you bring on yourself. We all do. Paul wrote of this kind of situation in 1 Thessalonians.

> **1 Thessalonians 3:1–2 NKJV**
> ¹ Therefore, when we could no longer endure it, we thought it good to be left in Athens alone,
> ² and sent Timothy, our brother and minister of God, and our fellow laborer in the gospel of Christ, to establish you and encourage you concerning your faith,
> ³ that no one should be shaken by these afflictions; for you yourselves know that we are appointed to this.

I'm sure the people in Thessalonica would rather have had Paul come, but Paul sent somebody else to take his place.

SOLUTION: GET ALONE WITH GOD

Paul's solution for distress was to get alone. Like any leader, he needed regular times of renewing his energy and perspective. If you don't do the same, you're going to crash.

To perform at your best, you need days of rest. Even Jesus needed rest. Jesus was so exhausted that in the middle of a storm He was sound asleep! He was fatigued because he faced the same kinds of things you and I face.

Jesus' solution and Paul's solution is our solution. I'll illustrate it with a story of a friend of mine named John. John was a pastor who began teaching on faith in his church. A couple of deacons didn't like "that faith stuff" message. They came to him and said, "A lot of people in the church are questioning whether you should be pastor because of your strong stand on this hyper-faith business. We want you to quit teaching 'faith' in this church and if you don't, we want you to leave. The whole board agrees with us."

John's response? Though he was a good leader, he got depressed. His distress was incredible. He came to Lansing and sought my advice. I told him, "Don't go home yet. Go to a hotel and get yourself a room and get alone with God. Listen for what God has to say about this situation and then just do it." God will tell you things when you cry out to him. He will tell you the truth about any situation you find yourself in.

Jeremiah 33:3a NKJV
"Call to Me, and I will answer you...."

John went into that hotel room thinking the whole church was against him and the whole board wanted him out. The next morning, he walked out of the hotel with confidence. He had heard from God. He went back to his church and the next Sunday he said, "Ladies and gentlemen, we're going to have a church business meeting tonight about whether or not you want me to continue as your pastor. Please come back tonight for this extremely important meeting."

Many people came back that night. John got up and said, "I've called you here tonight because of a problem these two deacons have brought to my attention." And he pointed to the two men as they began to squirm.

"They have told me that the church is against me, and the entire church board wants me to resign as pastor because I'm teaching about faith. So tonight we're going to vote. Do you want me to go, or do you want them to go?" The church voted and there were only four votes against the pastor, no doubt from those two deacons and their wives. As a result, they stormed out, never came back, and peace returned to the church. John became so popular that his peers elected him as presbyter for the whole section.

Are you facing distress as a leader? Get alone with God! Go to the beach or a mountaintop. Go somewhere. Get alone and get your perspective back. Or rather, get God's perspective inside you again.

I have a pastor friend who made a deal with a nearby hotel. He knew that some people check out early and their room isn't cleaned until noon. This pastor asked the hotel manager, "Could I use a room until the cleaning people get there?" The manager agreed, so he is able to use a free hotel room to get alone and seek God's mind in any situation.

SOLUTION: DELEGATE

The other thing Paul did was to appoint a delegate. Sure, everybody was crying, "We want Paul to preach! We want Paul to teach!"

But Paul said, "Look, I'm at the point where I can't handle any more. I'm so overburdened I feel like I'm on the brink of death, so I'm going to send Timothy. He'll be preaching and teaching for a while."

When I started in ministry, I did everything myself including tasks like tape duplication. The Lord told me, "You're robbing someone else of their ministry!" So I appointed a delegate. It is pride to think only you can do everything the right way. As a pacesetting leader you must learn to delegate! Moses learned this lesson; Paul did, too; even Jesus delegated. We will study this further in coming chapters.

SOLUTION: SEE GOD IN THE PROBLEM

Next, don't just see the storm, but see God in the storm. Jesus was in the boat and told the disciples, "We're going across." A storm came up, and the disciples were freaking out and full of distress. They started talking like men who were going to die. What did Jesus say? "Where is your faith? Peace, be still!" The storm calmed. He showed them what faith can do.[1]

God is somewhere in every situation. Sometimes we're too busy seeing the devil, the causes of agitation, the reasons for our distress. You can choose to see the devil in everything or you can choose to see God's hand and purpose. A leader should spend a lot more time looking up than looking down.

SOLUTION: CREATE AN ATMOSPHERE

Finally, when you're alone create an atmosphere for hearing from God. Play soft, soothing music. Make the room cozy and comfortable. Open a window for a soft breeze. Turn off the television and your cell phone. Make your surroundings conducive to relaxation so you can open your heart and mind to hear the Lord speak.

And when you have heard from him, and when your stress level is back to perfect—get back to work! If you are a business leader, start leading again. If you are a minister, start ministering again. If you are a parent, start parenting again! If you don't get back to work, you will drift into the "drone zone" of boredom and ineffectiveness. Jump back into the fray and get ready for greater victories as a pacesetting leader!

DEVOTIONAL REFLECTIONS

1: Which strategy for dealing with distress most appeals to you? Write down which one you feel you need to put into practice right now.

---

[1] Matthew 8

2: Are you in a time of too much, too little, or just enough stress? What indicators tell you this?

3: When was the last time you got alone with God? Make a regular appointment to spend time with him.

A pacesetting leader must develop teaching skills that will
motivate and inspire audiences.

23

HOW TO TEACH
EFFECTIVELY

S. Truett Cathy, one of the great Christian business leaders of the last hundred years, founded **Chick-fil-A**® restaurants, a massive, multibillion-dollar enterprise.[1] [2] But he also had another calling—Sunday school teacher. For all of his life, Cathy taught the Bible to thirteen-year-old boys at his local church. He never felt that being CEO and founder of Chick-fil-A® put him above the calling to teach others. Cathy also knew how to get a boy's attention—he built dirt bike paths on his property and let the boys ride around his estate. When they were energized and having fun, they were more open to learning about Jesus.

That is a great example of the leader's calling to teach and motivate others. As a pacesetting leader, you are called to teach and inspire people in various settings. The people may be your

---

[1] Cathy, S. Truett, *It's Easier to Succeed than to Fail*, Oliver Nelson Publishing, Alpharetta, GA, 30022, 1989.

[2] Cathy, S. Truett, *How Did You do it, Truett?: A Recipe for Success*, Looking Glass Publishing, Decatur, GA 30030, 2007.

employees, congregation members, children, grandchildren, Sunday School class, neighbors, or students. Teaching can happen one-on-one or in groups. But the Bible is very clear that leaders, and indeed all of God's people, are called to teach.

Jesus, the Great Teacher, loved teaching his disciples. To teach was one of the last directives he gave to his followers before he ascended to Heaven.

Matthew 28:19–20 NLT
[19] "Therefore, go and make disciples of all the nations, baptizing them in the name of the Father and the Son and the Holy Spirit.
[20] Teach these new disciples to obey all the commands I have given you. And be sure of this: I am with you always, even to the end of the age."

The writer to Hebrews taught that Christians should grow up and mature in knowledge of the Lord. You can't always be the "baby" receiving instructions on the basics; you need to grow up and learn how to handle the tougher, more complicated situations you face.

Hebrews 5:12–13 NLT
[12] You have been believers so long now that you ought to be teaching others. Instead, you need someone to teach you again the basic things about God's word. You are like babies who need milk and cannot eat solid food.
[13] For someone who lives on milk is still an infant and doesn't know how to do what is right.

Only infants aren't willing to teach others. Immature leaders are the ones who say, "I don't want to teach; I just want to be fed, and I only want to eat cream puffs! Don't teach me anything that will make me feel bad. I don't care if I—or others—know how to tell right from wrong."

Hebrews 5:14 NLT
Solid food is for those who are mature, who through training have the skill to recognize the difference between right and wrong.

DON'T BE A CREAM PUFF

Being a pacesetting leader means embracing the responsibility of teaching, motivating, and building others up along the way. It is time to quit being a creampuff and step up to your calling to teach! If you dread the thought of speaking in front of people, rest assured that you are not alone. When God appeared to Moses in the burning bush and called him to speak to Pharaoh, Moses said, "Oh, not me, I can't talk. I stutter."[3] But in the end he fulfilled his task and became a great leader. Jesus said,

Mark 9:23 NLT
"What do you mean, 'If I can'?" Jesus asked. "Anything is possible if a person believes."

Colossians 3:16 NJKV
Let the word of Christ dwell in you richly in all wisdom, teaching and admonishing one another in psalms and hymns and spiritual songs, singing with grace in your hearts to the Lord.

This is a general instruction for all believers. With the Holy Spirit working from within, you *can* teach others effectively.

Your job as a pacesetting leader is not to teach others in a grudging way but to communicate with excellence and make your teaching interesting. Some leaders have a great vision but never learn the art of communicating that vision to others. As a result, people don't receive their teaching and the vision dims. To lead well and help others bear fruit, you must impart your vision

---

[3] Exodus 4:10

to them in a way that captures their hearts and attention. I will share how to do that in the next few chapters.

THE PURPOSE OF TEACHING

Your goal in teaching is to motivate and inspire your listeners. You do this by educating them, giving them a method to apply the new knowledge in a practical way, inspiring them to change their attitudes and actions for the better, thereby causing them to mature. Let's look at each one.

1: Educate

When you have the opportunity to teach or share with people, be sure to educate your audience. Tell them something they don't know. Give them knowledge and wisdom, particularly from God's Word. The first objective in teaching is to impart knowledge.

> **Hosea 4:6 NKJV**
> My people are destroyed for lack of knowledge. Because you have rejected knowledge, I also will reject you from being priest for Me; Because you have forgotten the law of your God, I also will forget your children.

Knowledge is important. Without it people don't grow into mature Christians.

2: Give a practical application

Your teaching should always give people a way to apply the knowledge in a practical way. Have you ever been frustrated with preachers or teachers who tell you what you *ought* to do, but never tell you how to do it? We all need a practical application plan: Step 1; Step 2; Step 3, etc. Otherwise the teaching can never manifest as action. Here's what the Gospel record says about Jesus.

Mark 4:33-34 MSG
33-34 With many stories like these, he presented his message to them, fitting the stories to their experience and maturity. He was never without a story when he spoke. When he was alone with his disciples, he went over everything, sorting out the tangles, untying the knots.

Luke 24:27 AMP
Then beginning with Moses and [throughout] all the Prophets, He went on explaining and interpreting to them in all the Scriptures the things concerning and referring to Himself.

Jesus gave them application. He expounded on the teachings of the *Old Testament*. So we want to educate by giving knowledge and expounding on that knowledge in a practical way that people can apply.[4]

3: Cause a changed attitude

Next you want to cause an attitudinal change in people's minds and lives. If people believe they are victims, or if they have an entitlement mentality, or a scarcity mentality you want to change that attitude! You want to inspire an attitude that will result in different beliefs and different actions.

4: Bring to higher maturity

Finally, you want to bring people to a higher level of maturity. There's a time when we need milk, but then there's a time we move on to cereal and then T-bone steaks.

1 Peter 2:2-3 NLT
2 Like newborn babies, you must crave pure spiritual milk so that you will grow into a full experience of salvation. Cry out for this nourishment,
3 now that you have had a taste of the Lord's kindness.

---

[4] You may find *Turning Ordinary Talks into Heavenly Impartations* helpful. This CD and workbook set is available at www.davewilliams.com.

Ephesians 4:13–16 NLT

[13] This will continue until we all come to such unity in our faith and knowledge of God's Son that we will be mature in the Lord, measuring up to the full and complete standard of Christ.

[14] Then we will no longer be immature like children. We won't be tossed and blown about by every wind of new teaching. We will not be influenced when people try to trick us with lies so clever they sound like the truth.

[15] Instead, we will speak the truth in love, growing in every way more and more like Christ, who is the head of his body, the church.

[16] He makes the whole body fit together perfectly. As each part does its own special work, it helps the other parts grow, so that the whole body is healthy and growing and full of love.

Paul was saying, "We must teach and instruct until everybody becomes mature in Christ." We want to help people fit into God's program. We want them to find their gift, their passion, their place and fit them into it for the greatest results in God's Kingdom. That place may be in a business, school or church, but everyone has a place. Your goal as a leader is to help people mature and find their place through your influence and teaching.

You may have noticed that two preachers can preach the same sermon, but one seems to make it come alive. What's the difference? One has learned to teach motivationally and the other has not.

Next, I want to share with you some thoughts about teaching that will help you, a pacesetting leader, motivate people, change their attitudes and bring them into a higher maturity in Christ.

DEVOTIONAL REFLECTIONS

1: Do you see yourself as a teacher? Why or why not?

2: Who is someone who taught you and helped you mature? What was effective about his or her teaching?

3: What are opportunities to teach that you have right now?

Be prepared!

24

MAKE IT BURN

Luke 24:32 NKJV
And they said to one another, "Did not our heart burn within us while He talked with us on the road, and while He opened the Scriptures to us?"

I want to give you an easy-to-remember acronym for a basic rule of teaching: SOB—that means: Simple, Often, and Burn. Say it **simply**, say it **often**, make it **burn**!

The disciples on the road to Emmaus, after encountering the risen Lord, said, "Did not our hearts burn within us?" Jesus' teaching was simple and repetitive, and they recognized his teaching because it caused their hearts to burn within them.

Say it simply, say it often, and make it burn. Only the Holy Spirit can help you make it burn in people's hearts. Paul said,

1 Corinthians 2:4 NLT
And my message and my preaching were very plain. Rather than using clever and persuasive speeches, I relied only on the power of the Holy Spirit.

If you say it simply, the Holy Spirit will make those simple truths burn within the hearts of your listeners.

We must also say it often. Don't assume that everybody already knows everything. I can teach things seven times, and the eighth time people say, "Wow, that was powerful!" It took eight repetitions, but they finally got it!

SIMPLE STEPS TO MOTIVATE AND INFLUENCE

1: Communicate with your audience in a way they can understand

If you are preparing to speak to a group of engineers, learn a little about engineering so you can speak their language.

Nehemiah 8:12 MSG
So the people went off to feast, eating and drinking and including the poor in a great celebration. Now they got it; they understood the reading that had been given to them.

It's not enough to hear. People have to understand and relate to what you tell them. D. L. Moody once spoke to a group of pastors in San Francisco, and they asked, "What's the number one secret of your preaching?" He replied, "Preach plain."

We've all known people who try to impress us with big words. Nobody wants to bring their dictionary to look up words when you speak. Deepen your content but simplify your presentation. Don't go over people's heads just to make yourself look smart. Preach and teach plainly!

2: Don't talk too much

Proverbs 10:14 says that wise people treasure knowledge, but the babbling of a fool invites disaster. It is often true that the more words you use, the less effective and persuasive you will be. I have many uncompleted messages in my files because I get to point four of six points, and the Holy Spirit says, "That's enough.

I'll fill in the rest." I never feel like I have to get through all my notes. The point isn't the words, it's the purpose behind them.

3: Prepare

A baseball coach once said, "The will to win means nothing unless you have the will to prepare." I overheard a speaker say, "It took me twenty hours of preparation time to give that 'impromptu' speech that was so successful." You may make it *look* easy, but people don't see the effort that went into it behind the scenes. If you are willing to invest the time beforehand— the work, the sweat, the research, the organization—you will be rewarded openly when people's lives are changed. Preparing means knowing your subject.

> **2 Corinthians 11:6 NKJV**
> Even though I am untrained in speech, yet I am not in knowledge.

Some leaders try to teach without knowing their subject.

> **1 Timothy 1:7 NLT**
> They want to be known as teachers of the law of Moses, but they don't know what they are talking about, even though they speak so confidently."

There are some unprepared leaders who don't have a clue; yet they try to be teachers. They never put in the preparation or seek understanding. Exodus 12 talks about the critical time of preparation before the Passover. Part of the armor of God is the shoes of the preparation of the Gospel of peace.[1] Preparation is an important key if you want to be an inspiring, motivational, teacher able to impart great truths into the lives of others.

4: Be helpful in your talks; make sure the knowledge you give is helpful

---

[1] Ephesians 6:13–18

Acts 20:20b NKJV
...I kept back nothing that was helpful, but proclaimed it to you, and taught you publicly and from house to house.

Romans 12:6–8 MSG
[6–8] If you preach, just preach God's Message, nothing else; if you help, just help, don't take over; if you teach, stick to your teaching; if you give encouraging guidance, be careful that you don't get bossy; if you're put in charge, don't manipulate; if you're called to give aid to people in distress, keep your eyes open, be quick to respond; if you work with the disadvantaged, don't let yourself get irritated with them or depressed by them. Keep a smile on your face.

5: Use repetition

2 Peter 1:12–13, 15 NLT
[12] Therefore, I will always remind you about these things—even though you already know them and are standing firm in the truth you have been taught.
[13] And it is only right that I should keep on reminding you as long as I live.
[15] so I will work hard to make sure you always remember these things after I am gone.

Jesus said,

Matthew 13:52 NLT
"Every teacher of religious law who becomes a disciple in the Kingdom of Heaven is like a homeowner who brings from his storeroom new gems of truth as well as old."

This is part of the SOB we looked at earlier. Say it simple, say it often, and make it burn. Repetition works.

SECRET STRENGTHS OF GOOD TEACHING

1: Be guided by God

Make sure you are listening to God.

Jeremiah 1:17a NLT
"Get up and prepare for action. Go out and tell them
everything I tell you to say. Do not be afraid of them, or I will
make you look foolish in front of them...."

John 16:29–30 NLT
[29] Then his disciples said, "At last you are speaking plainly
and not figuratively.
[30] Now we understand that you know everything, and there's
no need to question you. From this we believe that you
came from God."

The disciples became convinced and your listeners will, too,
when they realize you are being guided by God.

2: Pray! Pray! Pray!

2 Corinthians 3:5 NLT
It is not that we think we are qualified to do anything on our
own. Our qualification comes from God.

Whether we are teaching or leading in an area we know well
or not, our qualification comes from God, so we had better talk
to him first. Jesus said you'll get an open reward for private prayer.

Matthew 6:6 NLT
But when you pray, go away by yourself, shut the door
behind you, and pray to your Father in private. Then your
Father, who sees everything, will reward you.

St. Paul said our power and success only comes from God.
This is why I don't go to preach anywhere without taking intercessors with me. I need people praying for me. It's no wonder
good things happen as a result.

I tell the intercessors, "I'm going to prepare, I'm going to be
guided by God, I'm going to do my part, but you prayer partners are the ones who really lift the experience up." When people
come to Christ, get filled with the Holy Spirit, and get healed,

and when teaching goes forth and is received in power, it's because somebody is praying.

Years ago, a man from a Bible college came and asked, "Pastor, how do you go about preparing for a sermon?"

I answered, "The first thing I do is pray and ask, 'God, what do I need to say that will help the greatest number of people? What's on your heart, that I can share with them?'"

The young man responded, "That's the stupidest thing I've ever heard of in my life. You've got the Word, any of it'll preach!" Perhaps that is so, but not just "any" of it will cause people's hearts to burn within them unless it's directed from the Holy Spirit for that moment or season. I don't mean to be disrespectful to that man, but all the while I have taught God's Word, he has served beer and pizza in a pizzeria. It's not just your education that's going to make you effective. You have to hear from God!

3: Be openly enthusiastic about your material

Get excited! Here's what Paul said...

Romans 12:11 NLT
Never be lazy, but work hard and serve the Lord enthusiastically.

Get excited about your topic and people will listen much more eagerly. When I was in engineering school the instructor walked in one day and said, "I hope none of you feel like learning today, 'cause I sure don't feel like teaching." Do you think we felt like learning from him? No! Your listeners will reflect your attitude. If you are motivated by what you teach, they will be, too.

4: Speak with authority

Jesus spoke with authority, not as the scribes and the Pharisees did. Teachers must speak with authority, not in a wishy-washy way. When you have prayed, studied, and prepared properly you will speak with a true leader's authority.

5: Use illustrations and testimonies

Personal illustrations bring application to your message. They enliven knowledge and color what might otherwise be a drab picture. Put some experience around the points you are making, and don't be afraid of using personal illustrations. Jesus did. Say it simple, say it often and make it burn!

6: Remember W-I-I-F-M?

I mentioned **What's In It For Me?** in an earlier chapter. Everyone wants the answer to that question. Always help people understand the benefits they will receive when they apply your teaching in their lives. Even if it's a tough teaching, you can convey the benefits in such a way that people want to get on board.

> **Matthew 16:24b NKJV**
> ..."If anyone desires to come after Me, let him deny himself, and take up his cross, and follow Me."

On the face of it, that doesn't seem like a very attractive proposition! But what are the benefits of denying your self, taking up your cross and following Jesus? Well, there's eternal life, a bountiful harvest of righteousness, and *much* more.

In a business or family setting, you may be talking about difficult choices you have to make or changes that are coming. Make sure to get across the benefits involved in those changes. People shouldn't be wondering, "What's in it for me?" because you will have already told them.

7: Talk to one person

Pretend you are speaking to one individual, not a group. Don't say things like, "Friends, hear me now!" Or, "Listen, church!" Once you do that, you're talking to no one. If you want your message to be effective and to burn, speak as if you are speaking to one person. Everyone in the audience will think, *he's talking to me!*

8: Avoid worn out phrases and wordiness

Don't let clichés and wordiness clutter up your message. Some leaders use phrases like, "each and every one of you." That's too much. Just say, "each of you." Every time you add words and expressions where you don't need to, you weaken the message. For example, I have heard leaders say, "I want every single person in this room to stand." Why put the word "single" in there? Is he talking to unmarried people? Just drop the word "single." Others say things like, "I'm really, really, really excited about this!" They don't understand that they lose power with all the repetitions. If you want to use a word like really or very say it once and let it stand.

We've all been in services where the preacher said, "Amen, we're going to open our Bibles, hallelujah, to John chapter three, glory to God! Praise Jesus! We're going to talk about a verse, hallelujah, that we all know, praise God, verse sixteen." Wow! It's hard to find the point in the midst of all those hallelujahs and glories. The same goes for any teaching environment.

Your job is to impart something to people. Be very careful with the words you use and don't distract from your purpose by using "non-words" or filler phrases. It's annoying, and you're pulling the plug on the connection you have with your audience.

In the next chapter, I'll share brief but effective ways to organize your message for maximum impact.

DEVOTIONAL REFLECTIONS

1: Briefly jot down each of the points in this chapter to help you remember how to teach effectively.

2: What are your areas of strength as a teacher? What are areas of weakness?

3: How can you become a more effective teacher where you are serving now? Which of these strategies stands out to you?

God has given you an awesome mandate
to teach and share valuable principles
with others.

25
CHAPTER

HOW TO ORGANIZE
YOUR MESSAGE

God is a God of order. He placed order in all of creation. I laugh when people say, "I don't believe in organized religion." What do they believe in, disorganized religion? There's order in the Body of Christ—the Christian church. A body in disorder is diseased. As a pacesetting leader, your messages must have order.

How do you organize a motivational teaching? In a ministry setting, you should start with a Bible text. This lets the listener know what biblical principles you are going to be imparting. You can't grab a theme out of the air. You must start from God's Word. It's true in other settings as well. You should define your purpose early so everyone knows where you are taking them and what you want to impart.

1: Introduction

Start with an introduction that grabs their attention and makes your audience want to listen to the rest of the message.

Your introduction can be a question like, "Are you suffering from the darkness of depression, as so many are these days? Today I'm going to impart God's miracle solution to depression that he has laid out clearly in his Word." People's interest will be piqued with a clear introduction like that.

As a business leader you might say, "Are you interested in advancing your career wherever you work throughout your life? Today I'm going to show you how to rise to the top under in any situation and under any circumstance."

In your introduction, you might use a story or a question that ties in and applies to your message. If you go the humorous route, don't use humor that someone might be uncomfortable with or find offensive. Also, there's no need to preface a joke with something like, "I heard this joke." A large part of humor comes from the element of surprise. If you tell people it's a joke, they'll sit there waiting for the punch line, and the line will lose its punch when it comes.

There are plenty of funny true stories, too. Once, I was talking about solving challenging problems, and I told the story about a bunch of school girls who started wearing lipstick and got into the habit of blotting their lips on the girls' bathroom mirror. It was hard for the janitor to clean the mess off, so finally they took the girls into the rest room and said, "We want to show you how hard it is to clean these lipstick marks off the mirror." They put a squeegee in the toilet, swished it around and started cleaning the mirror! None of the girls thought it was a good idea to kiss the mirror anymore. Problem solved!

Genuine laughter opens people's ears to hear what you say. If you do it right, humor is very effective to start your message.

2: Body

After your introductory remarks, you move into the body of your message. This includes the main points, applications, illustrations and authoritative support. The support may come from the Bible or from experts. You have several choices of how to approach your subject.

- You can give a message of one to five points; make sure you don't go much over that or people will start forgetting what you said
- You can make one point and hit it from three or four angles using illustrations and applications
- You can expound on a specific text from the Bible, and go through it line-by-line

I love these methods because you delve deep into the meaning and come up with riches.

- Make a list

This is one of my favorite methods for organizing the body of a message. I have a CD message called *Twenty-One Things I've Learned in Sixty-Two Years*. These messages are fun and energetic. You spend a couple of minutes on each point. You can find examples of this kind of teaching in the Bible. Peter did a "list" sermon.

2 Peter 1:5–7 NKJV
5 But also for this very reason, giving all diligence, add to your faith virtue, to virtue knowledge,
6 to knowledge self-control, to self-control perseverance, to perseverance godliness,
7 to godliness brotherly kindness, and to brotherly kindness love.

- Use a "Problem-Solution" format

Paul did this when writing about the end times. You paint a dark picture—the problem. John explained how terrible it's going to be on the earth during the tribulation. Jesus did the same thing. First, you show the problem, then you give the good news of the solution. When you offer a biblical, practical solution, you will find that people respond.

- **Extemporaneous sermons**

This where you go in with no definite plan. This should be a rare practice. I can remember only two times I have spoken extemporaneously in my whole thirty-plus years of teaching.

I remember coming to church at 5 a.m. one Sunday morning, and as I was driving down the highway, the Lord said, "I don't want you to preach the message you planned. I've got something else I want you to speak about." The sense of God's presence was so strong that I pulled off on the side of the road. He simply said, "Now is the day of salvation." That's all he gave me to go on. I stepped into that pulpit that Sunday morning and said, "Today, my text is, 'Now is the day of salvation.'" I had no idea what I was going to say next. I found myself going all the way back to Adam and Eve. Then I covered the doctrine of Christ and what the prophets said about Jesus. Then I gave an altar call. That Sunday morning more than 300 people came forward to receive Christ as their Savior!

I *never* plan to speak extemporaneously, but when the Lord directs me this way, it is powerful.

3: Conclusion

The last part of your message is the conclusion. Successful conclusions can be done in a number of ways. Many speakers conclude by repeating their points, which is fine. Some end with a story. I encourage you as a pacesetting leader to take it to the next level and consider giving some sort of a call to action. Let people know how you want them to change their lives. You don't have to do it every time so that it becomes repetitive, but giving people an assignment can effectively move them to their own next level of leadership.

Be positive in your conclusion. End on an up note. Don't leave people on an emotional or spiritual low, especially if you have addressed a difficult subject.

God has given you an awesome mandate to teach and share valuable principles with others. Your assignment now is to watch other leaders, communicators, preachers, and teachers. Take notes and observe exactly how they organize their message. What outline did he or she use? How many illustrations? What was the application and call to action? How did he or she start and end the message? I have notes from other preachers that go back to 1975. As I studied how other preachers communicated effectively, my own abilities grew. That kind of study will help you prepare messages that are educational, inspirational, motivational, applicable, and impartational. You can do it!

DEVOTIONAL REFLECTIONS

1: **What type of introduction attracts you: a humorous story; an idea that provokes your interest; a simple explanation of your teaching?**

2: **Take some time to prepare a message using one of the approaches suggested above.**

Do you want a life of no runs, no hits, no errors? No way! Pacesetting leaders aren't afraid to take a swing and play the game.

26

BREAK BARRIERS & OVERCOME OBSTACLES

As a kid playing in the back yard one day, I heard a loud boom come from the sky. It sounded like thunder, but it wasn't. The sound was made by a jet breaking the sound barrier that created a sonic boom. The first person to do that was test pilot, Chuck Yeager, in 1947. Against the fearful predictions of many experts, Yeager survived the experience and went on to have a long career in aviation. Breaking that "unbreakable" barrier became one of the most celebrated events of the aviation age.

Barriers and obstacles pop up in your life whenever you pursue vision and goals. Often when you have a promise or vision from God, you think it's going to be smooth sailing. I can assure you that the opposite is true! A legitimate stage of any venture in business, ministry, marriage, or life is the obstacle stage.

Unfortunately, this is the stage where many leaders quit. You've probably heard the adage, "Quitters never win, and winners never quit." How true! Barriers, obstacles, and roadblocks are meant to be moved by a pacesetting leader. They are put there to enlarge you, to draw out your faith and tenacity. Pacesetting leaders see doors when others see walls.

Hebrews 6:11–12 NKJV
[11] And we desire that each one of you show the same diligence to the full assurance of hope until the end,
[12] that you do not become sluggish, but imitate those who through faith and patience inherit the promises.

I'm sure you have probably heard of Thomas A. Edison, Ronald Reagan, George Washington, Abraham Lincoln, Martin Luther King Jr., Arthur J. Pendergrass. Who? Arthur J. Pendergrass! You never heard of Arthur J. Pendergrass? That's because he's the one who quit.

Your vision will only become a reality through faith and perseverance. It will not be smooth sailing, but you will make it!

BREAKING THROUGH

Barriers are meant to be broken. Obstacles are meant to be overcome. The writer of this psalm saw a door not a barrier!

Psalm 138:7 NKJV
Though I walk in the midst of trouble, You will revive me; You will stretch out Your hand Against the wrath of my enemies, And Your right hand will save me.

Obstacles can develop your character and competency if you let them. Character is who you are—your traits, values, morals, honesty, and courage; competency is how well you do what you do. Character is the leading indicator of genuine success, fruitfulness, and effectiveness in a leader's life. Character shines brightest in the midst of difficulty.

James 1:2–4 MSG
[2-4] Consider it a sheer gift, friends, when tests and challenges come at you from all sides. You know that under pressure, your faith-life is forced into the open and shows its true

colors. So don't try to get out of anything prematurely. Let it do its work so you become mature and well-developed, not deficient in any way.

A pastor in California once told me, "I know you get kicked when you're in the ministry, but I always determine the direction they kick me!" When you get kicked, you can determine to be kicked forward, not backwards. I call this character trait "patient determination." You are determined and you are patient. You are determined that every obstacle will not set you back but move you ahead.

When Oswald J. Smith had a vision of being a missionary and winning people to Jesus in foreign lands, he was rejected by the missions board of his denomination. So, what did he do? He determined the direction of the kick. He started a great church in Canada and trained hundreds of missionaries. Even though Oswald J. Smith did not become a missionary, he became one of the greatest missionary trainers in history.

Paul also confronted obstacles in his life and ministry. In his letter to the Corinthians he described how he faced adversity.

2 Corinthians 4:8–11 NLT

[8] We are pressed on every side by troubles, but we are not crushed. We are perplexed, but not driven to despair.
[9] We are hunted down, but never abandoned by God. We get knocked down, but we are not destroyed.
[10] Through suffering, our bodies continue to share in the death of Jesus so that the life of Jesus may also be seen in our bodies.
[11] Yes, we live under constant danger of death because we serve Jesus, so that the life of Jesus will be evident in our dying bodies.

2 Corinthians 4:16–18 NLT

[16] That is why we never give up. Though our bodies are dying, our spirits are being renewed every day.

¹⁷ For our present troubles are small and won't last very long. Yet they produce for us a glory that vastly outweighs them and will last forever!
¹⁸ So we don't look at the troubles we can see now; rather, we fix our gaze on things that cannot be seen. For the things we see now will soon be gone, but the things we cannot see will last forever.

As a pacesetting leader you should welcome obstacles. The greatest leaders are the ones who face the greatest obstacles. Think of the people in history that we admire most. Every one faced major challenges and led others through them.

In leadership, you will face challenges, hardship, risk, adversity, bad breaks, unfairness, difficulties, and reversals. Sometimes you will suffer anguish as a leader, you will feel tormented and confronted. There will be protests, demands, misunderstood motives, antagonism, interference, interruption, obstructions, barriers, hindrances, distractions, negative comments, stumbling blocks, and ditches. What will you do when you encounter these things?

As a pacesetting leader, you focus on your vision and direction. You will see doors when others see walls. You will develop a callousness to defeat. You understand the reason for obstacles—problems always precede advancement. I'm convinced that many people stop just shy of their miracle. They give up just moments before their miracle was scheduled to arrive.

King David was enlarged and advanced when he came upon trouble, barriers, obstacles, resistance, and misunderstandings. Those things always appear before a miracle breakthrough. Tenacity, faithfulness, hang-in-there power is the bridge between the calling and the choosing.

Psalm 4:1 AMP
Answer me when I call, O God of my righteousness (uprightness, justice, and right standing with You)! You have freed

me when I was hemmed in and enlarged me when I was in distress; have mercy upon me and hear my prayer.

WHERE OBSTACLES COME FROM

Some obstacles you face will be self-imposed. They are usually barriers that exist only in your mind, and are usually motivated by fear. For example, any time you share a big vision with someone, he or she will inevitably tell you all the problems you will face. Preacher J. Vernon McGee told of an epitaph in a graveyard that read: "Here lay the bones of Miss Betsy Jones. She wanted no problems; she wanted no terrors. So she lived an old maid and died an old maid; no runs, no hits, no errors."

Do you want a life of no runs, no hits, no errors? No way! Pacesetting leaders aren't afraid to take a swing and play the game. When you enter the fray you will make mistakes, but if you don't try you can't succeed. Babe Ruth, the home run king, was also the strikeout king. He struck out more than any other baseball player of his time. But he is remembered best for the home runs. You cannot worry about what people might think.

Psalm 118:6 KJV
The Lord is on my side; I will not fear: what can man do unto me?

Proverbs 29:25 AMP
The fear of human opinion disables; trusting in God protects you from that.

Many people don't come to Christ because they're afraid of what someone else might think. They worry what their spouse or friends might think, and so they never choose Jesus!

Others have failed at something before, and that failure caused a barrier to form in their minds. He or she will say, "I don't want to try that because I'm afraid I'll fail again." When fear of failure troubles me, I like to read Isaiah.

Isaiah 43:18–19 NKJV
[18] "Do not remember the former things, Nor consider the things of old.
[19] Behold, I will do a new thing, Now it shall spring forth; Shall you not know it? I will even make a road in the wilderness And rivers in the desert."

You may have failed in the past; we all have. Your past doesn't determine your future unless you let it!

2 Corinthians 5:17 NKJV
Therefore if any man be in Christ, he is a new creature: old things are passed away; behold, all things are become new.

Some fear they are not perfect enough to overcome problems. He or she thinks, *as soon as I develop this quality or learn this or quit doing that, I will be ready to succeed.*

Ecclesiastes 11:4 NLT
Farmers who wait for perfect weather never plant. If they watch every cloud, they never harvest.

Ecclesiastes 11:14 GNT
If you wait until the wind and the weather are just right, you will never plant anything and never harvest anything.

No matter what I've accomplished in my life, someone has told me it was the wrong time to do it. You will always hear someone say, "It's not the right time." Learn to rejoice when you hear those words! You've just encountered an obstacle that you will, with God's help, overcome.

DON'T WAIT FOR PERFECT CONDITIONS

A man was called to the ministry and said, "I'm going to answer that call, but first I've got to get a *Strong's Concordance.*" He worked at a gas station, saving money to get a this important reference book. After he accomplished that goal he said, "I can't launch into the ministry until I get a pulpit commentary.

Every good pastor has a pulpit commentary." He finally saved up enough money to get a pulpit commentary, and then he said, "All good preachers have a black suit." So, he saved for a black suit. Then there was something else and then something else. Finally he grew old and retired from the gas station and said, "I'm too old to answer that call to ministry."

Conditions and preparation do not need to be perfect for you to succeed. Whenever you try something new, you will fall down a few times. God expects that! Think of a baby beginning to walk. Think of when you learned to ride a two-wheel bike. Pacesetting leaders make mistakes, but they learn and improve by them. They get up, dust off their knees, and never quit. They develop and maintain a strong sense of Christ centered-ness.

2 Corinthians 3:5 NLT
It is not that we think we are qualified to do anything on our own. Our qualification comes from God.

We know that God working with us is what brings power, success, and influence in our leadership.

YOU CAN DO IT

Leadership can be a lonely, vulnerable place. No matter what vision you have, what goals you are pursuing, what dream is in your heart, you will face naysayers. They will say, "You can't do it because of this or that reason." I like this poem by Edgar Guest.[1]

It Couldn't Be Done

Somebody said that it couldn't be done,
But, he with a chuckle replied
That maybe it couldn't, but he would be one
Who wouldn't say so till he'd tried.

---

[1] *Collected Verse by Edgar Guest*, Buccaneer Books, Cutchogue, NY, 1976, page 285.

So he buckled right in with the trace of a grin
On his face. If he worried he hid it.
Then he started to sing as he tackled the thing
That couldn't be done, and he did it."
There are thousands to tell you it cannot be done
There are thousands to prophesy failure.
There are thousands to point out to you one by one
The dangers that wait to assail you.
But just buckle in with a bit of a grin,
Just take off your coat and go to it
Just start to sing as you tackle the thing
That "cannot be done," and you'll do it.

If you try to please everybody all the time, you'll end up pleasing nobody! You only have to please God, and the applause of Heaven is all you need. Usually those who do the most are criticized by those who do the least.

Set your mind and heart to be the pacesetting leader God has called you to be, and you won't quit when those inevitable obstacles come. Next we will look at some common responses—both good and bad—to obstacles.

DEVOTIONAL REFLECTIONS

1: What obstacles have you faced in your leadership? List some.

2: How did you overcome them? Did you fail to overcome any one of them?

3: What has been the result in your character of breaking through barriers?

Barriers and obstacles pop up in your life whenever you have a vision and goals.

Remember the frogs!

27

RESPONSES TO OBSTACLES

People respond in different ways to the obstacles they face. Some responses are negative and some are positive. The way you respond to obstacles determines your success.

WRONG RESPONSES TO OBSTACLES

1: Withdrawing

Some respond by withdrawing from the situation. This is what the demon-possessed man did in Jesus' day. He withdrew to the cemetery where nobody could bother him. People pull the covers over their heads and hide in the face of distressing situations. They want to check out of life.

When I became a pastor, I went through the old membership files and found a woman's name I didn't recognize. At that time, we had 125 members and 226 attendees so I pretty much knew everyone, but this name was unfamiliar.

I called the woman and said, "Hi, this is Pastor Williams from Mount Hope Church calling."

She immediately replied, "Aw, what do you want? I haven't been to that church in seven years and I'll never come back!"

"What happened?" I asked.

"You don't know what that song leader said to me. I've been bitter ever since."

"Would you like to give us another try?"

"I can't," she said. "I'm so full of arthritis I can hardly move."

This woman had withdrawn in the face of a relational obstacle she experienced at the church. What was the result? She was bitter and her body was literally breaking down due to her unforgiving attitude. She had withdrawn from an obstacle and fallen into ill health.

2: Misunderstanding

Another man told me he left the church because somebody on the platform gave him a dirty look one day. Talk about a *tiny* obstacle! Yet that perceived slight wrote this man's future.

I can tell you from experience, you should not read too much into people's looks. One of our staff pastors was preaching one Sunday, and I was sitting in the front row. I had a kink in my neck and it was hurting. I grimaced and shrugged my shoulders to get some relief. Later that week this pastor came to me and asked, "Did you have a problem with something I said last Sunday?"

I replied, "No! It was a great message."

"I saw a look on your face that concerned me." I remembered the kink in my neck that had made me grimace. It was a good thing this pastor didn't take offense and withdraw from the problem, and I was able to give him an explanation that eased his mind.

3: Substituting original goals for new goals

Another improper response to obstacles is to substitute new goals for the original ones. You might be tempted to say, "That promise didn't work out so I'm going to go after something else."

I tell people to be consistent. Remember, don't shoot at rabbits if you're hunting for quail. Don't substitute your goals, because that creates a double-minded situation and instability. James said the double-minded person can expect nothing from God

James 1:7–8 NKJV
7 For let not that man suppose that he will receive anything from the Lord;

8 he is a double-minded man, unstable in all his ways.

4: Becoming defensive

Another reaction to obstacles is to get defensive. For some years Rex Humbard, pastor of Cathedral of Tomorrow in Akron, Ohio, was reaching more people for Christ by radio and television than anyone else. He dedicated one of our new Mount Hope Church facilities years ago. But one of the ministers in Akron, who also had a radio program, spoke against Rex. He said, "Rex Humbard will shake your hand with his right hand while he picks your pocket with his left. Nobody's ever been healed there. If anybody can prove they have been healed over there, I will give them $5,000." People started taking him up on his offer, bringing verifiable medical evidence of healing. Of course, this pastor never paid anyone $5,000.

When news got back to Rex about what this minister said, Rex did not get defensive. He simply said, "I don't know why that brother would say something like that." He continued to treat him like a brother, even though this man treated Rex like an enemy. What a great example! If someone attacks you, don't get defensive, just trust the Lord to defend you.

5: Blaming others

Some leaders become overbearing and difficult to get along with when they face obstacles. I've known people who encounter a difficult season and start blaming everybody around them. I constantly hear other pastors place blame when they are having a difficult time. "This town has a strong Catholic influence, so there's not much chance of having a successful church." "The former pastor turned people off in this community, so there's no chance of having a successful church." Wrong! If God gives the vision, then success is guaranteed if you persevere through the challenges.

The most successful pastor I have ever known has just sixty-seven members in his church. He's my hero, and I would go to him for advice and counsel any day. Why? Because he's in a town with a population of sixty! The entire town attends his church, plus seven people from out of town! He made no excuses about his town being small. What a great example of pacesetting leadership right where God has placed you.

RIGHT RESPONSES TO OBSTACLES

1: Double-check your direction

It's okay, even desirable, to go to God and ask, "Is this vision from you? Am I doing my own thing—trying to build my own empire—or am I working with you in this situation? Am I going in the right direction?" I have found that sometimes I may need to take a little detour when I face an obstacle. At times God wants to take me around it to get to the other side. God guides me as I go. I call it "guidance on the go."

In my early years of ministry I faced an onslaught of obstacles that caused me to think, *maybe God didn't call me to be pastor.* The only place I could go to be alone was an old, smelly boiler room. I would go down there and pray, "God, I'm not coming out of this boiler room until I hear from you." I double-checked my direction, and when I came out of that boiler room I knew for certain what direction God wanted me to take. Then I could say with confidence, "I have heard from God. I know this is the right direction."

2: Put your hand to the plow

Obstacles give you an opportunity to fully commit to seeing the vision fulfilled. When facing trouble, some people make the mistake of focusing on their weaknesses. We all have weaknesses, but it doesn't pay to focus on them because that makes them grow in our sight. God gave you certain gifts and strengths, and he intends for you to build upon them. If you're constantly focusing on the weakness, you're not developing your God-given strengths. So regardless of your perceived weaknesses, keep pressing forward.

A man was having his boss over for dinner and he kept telling his wife, "The boss is self-conscious about his beaky nose! Whatever you do, don't say anything about his nose." So, his wife kept thinking to herself, "Don't say anything about his nose." As she was serving coffee that evening, she asked, "How many spoons of sugar would you like in your nose? I mean your coffee."

What you focus on fills your mind! God will take care of your weaknesses. Focus on your strengths. Put your hand to the plow and fully commit to making the vision a reality.

3: A steady pace brings prosperity

Luke 8:15 AMP
But as for that [seed] in the good soil, these are [the people] who, hearing the Word, hold it fast in a just noble, virtuous) and worthy heart, and steadily bring forth fruit with patience.

This is what leadership often is: it's day-in, day-out, steadily moving forward. As a pacesetting leader you don't pay attention to distractions to the left or right. Instead you cast all your cares on Jesus because he cares for you.

1 Peter 5:7 NLT
Give all your worries and cares to God, for he cares about you.

When you face a barrier or problem you are able to say, "I don't care." Because you know God is taking care of the problem for you, and it feels good! Jesus said there's only one thing worth being concerned about...sitting at his feet!

Luke 10:41–42 NLT

[41] The Lord answered her, "Martha, Martha! You are worried and troubled over so many things,

[42] but just one is needed. Mary has chosen the right thing, and it will not be taken away from her."

John Garlock gave one of the most powerful messages I've ever heard in my life at **Christ For The Nations Institute**. He was speaking on the subject of tenacity, and told the story about Shammah and the pea patch.

2 Samuel 23:11–12 NLT

[11] One time the Philistines gathered at Lehi and attacked the Israelites in a field full of lentils. The Israelite army fled,

[12] but Shammah held his ground in the middle of the field and beat back the Philistines. So the Lord brought about a great victory.

Shammah became one of the three most elite warriors in David's army—one of David's mighty men. In the face of great adversity, when everyone else had fled, Shammah did not give up. He stood his ground, and his faithfulness was rewarded. Promotion comes to those who hang in there. Garlock then shared this poem:

Two Frogs In Cream[1]

Two frogs fell into a can of cream,
Or so I've heard it told;
The sides of the can were shiny & steep,
The cream was deep & cold.

---

[1] Hamlett, T.C.

"O, what's the use?" croaked Number One,
"'Tis fate; no help's around.
Goodbye, my friends! Goodbye, sad world!"
And weeping still, he drowned.
But Number Two, of sterner stuff,
Dog-paddled in surprise.
The while he wiped his creamy face
And dried his creamy eyes.
"I'll swim awhile, at least," he said—
Or so I've heard he said—
"It really wouldn't help the world
If one more frog were dead."
An hour or two he kicked & swam,
Not once he stopped to mutter,
But kicked & kicked & swam & kicked,
and then hopped out...
On fresh churned butter.

There is great power in hanging in there. Cast your cares on God, move steadily forward and he will help you past the obstacles and barriers you will certainly face as a leader.

DEVOTIONAL REFLECTIONS

1: What negative responses have you observed in yourself when you face obstacles? List a few.

2: Do you feel the need to check your direction now, or is this a time of steady plodding?

3: Focus for a moment on the strengths in your leadership. Let the weaknesses fade from your mind as you get fresh vision for where you are heading.

Jesus taught the extra mile principle, and following it will radically revolutionize your life.

28
CHAPTER

THE EXTRA MILE
PRINCIPLE

A pacesetting leader is an enemy of "average." Whenever you feel like you are treading water and not moving ahead, it usually means you have settled into average, mediocre, and lukewarm. Jesus had something to say about lukewarm people.

Revelation 3:15–16 NLT
[15] "I know all the things you do, that you are neither hot nor cold. I wish that you were one or the other!
[16] But since you are like lukewarm water, neither hot nor cold, I will spit you out of my mouth!"

For any advancing leader, average is a dangerous place.

- **Average is the top of the bottom**
- **Average is the best of the worst**
- **Average is the bottom of the top**
- **Average is the worst of the best**

God has called you to be a leader of a different stripe. He has called you to go the extra mile. Jesus said:

Matthew 7:13–14 NKJV

[13] "Enter by the narrow gate; for wide is the gate and broad is the way that leads to destruction, and there are many who go in by it.
[14] Because narrow is the gate and difficult is the way which leads to life, and there are few who find it."

This is used as a soul-winning verse, which is fine, but Jesus didn't actually talk about heaven and hell in these verses. He said broad is the way to *destruction*. Narrow is the way to *life*. Yes, it can be used in the context of heaven and hell, but the principle also has a wider application. Jesus told us there is a broad way of doing things that leads to failure and destruction; there is a narrow way of doing things that leads to life and success.

Jesus taught the extra mile principle, and following it will radically revolutionize your life.

Matthew 5:41 NKJV
And whoever compels you to go one mile, go with him two.

What does this mean? In that day, it was lawful for a Roman soldier to grab a Jew and compel him to carry the soldier's gear for one mile—but not *more* than one mile. But Jesus' surprising statement gave a brand new, unheard of principle of success! He said, "Do more than you are compelled to do and do it with a good attitude!"

Remember, the Jews and Romans were enemies, and here was Jesus telling them to not only do what was required by the law, but to freely choose to go an extra mile. Then—and now—most people would say, "Are you nuts? Only a fool does more than he's paid to do. I'm punching in at nine and leaving at five. Even if I'm in the middle of something. I'm not going to give my job any more effort unless I'm paid to do it!"

However, Jesus, the Master Teacher, had a different perspective. In that same book of Matthew, chapter five, he taught many revolutionary principles. If a man takes your shirt, give him your jacket. If you are struck on the cheek, offer your other one. If you have to go one mile, go two. This is the extra mile principle.

St. Paul said:

1 Corinthians 9:24 NLT
Don't you realize that in a race everyone runs, but only one person gets the prize? So run to win!

If you don't win the race, you are an average "also-ran," common, mediocre. Failures don't do one thing more than they have to—but pacesetting leaders do. Nothing will advance your life more than the extra mile principle.

HOW TO HIT HIGHER LEVELS

When Tom Landry was coach of the Dallas Cowboys, someone asked him what was the difference between an NFL player and an All-Pro NFL player. Landry said, "There's not that much difference. It's certainly not ability, because they all have the ability to be an All-Pro player. The NFL is full of people with abilities and talents. The only difference is a little more drive, a little more determination, and a little more application."

By going the extra mile, some players rise to much higher levels of success and make a lot more money than other players—even if they have the same or just a little more talent.

In 1997, professional baseball players who batted .250, three hits out of twelve at bats, earned between $150,000 and $1.3 million a year. Those who batted .333, four hits out of twelve at bats, made $9 million. Just one more hit in twelve at bats made the difference between an average professional player and a very highly paid MVP. Here is another biblical example of the extra mile principle.

> **1 Chronicles 12:2a, 14 NLT**
> ² All of them were expert archers, and they could shoot arrows or sling stones with their left hand as well as their right.
> ¹⁴ These warriors from Gad were army commanders. The weakest among them could take on a hundred regular troops, and the strongest could take on a thousand!

I have read and studied those verses wondering what made these warriors a hundred to a thousand times better than the other soldiers. There's only one difference I can see in this passage that gives a hint: They learned to fight with their left hand as well as their right. They went beyond the average soldier who could fight with either the left or the right hand. They went the extra mile and trained to be proficient with both hands and that gave them an advantage a hundred to a thousand times greater than the average warrior.

Why settle for just average? Why not go the extra mile? Why not pick up an extra skill? Why not learn that new information? Why not practice just a little longer?

The other day, I went out to lunch. After eating, I walked up to the cash register. The cashier said in a bored, disinterested tone, "What can I do for you?" She treated me like I was an intrusion in her day. I would much rather go to a business where they give me a smile and say, "Mr. Williams, good to see you!" It is harder to be lazy than it is to be a hard worker. It is work to try to get out of work!

J.C. Penney was a wonderful Christian man. When he founded his stores he said, "We want to give our customers the best quality goods at the lowest price. I want every woman treated as if she were your mother, sister, or daughter. Every man that comes in, I want treated as your father, your brother, or your son." He respected the customer. He gave the customer more for their money than any other store, and J.C. Penney grew into a global chain.

In the Bible, Daniel and his three friends were ten times wiser than everybody else

Daniel 1:20 NLT
Whenever the king consulted them in any matter requiring wisdom and balanced judgment, he found them ten times more capable than any of the magicians and enchanters in his entire kingdom.

All they did was exercise just a little more obedience than the rest by refusing to eat food and drink that was not acceptable, and God blessed them with knowledge and favor. They refused meat and cake and pie, probably for a season, and were recognized as ten times greater.

How much more could you advance if you took little steps that bring big results?

BETTER BUSINESS

One way of advancing is to look for ways of improving your organization, ministry, or business—even if you are not the owner. You might work for a big company and you don't even know the CEO. But, if you continually look for ways of improving your efficiency and effectiveness you will be noticed in a good way and rewarded!

A young man worked as a clerk in a hardware store where some of items weren't selling. The boss said, "These products are just taking up room. Take them out and throw them away."

This young man thought, "How can I go the extra mile? How can I do something that others might not do? What can I do to help this situation?" So, he set up card tables in the middle of the store and put the stuff that wasn't selling on them. He made a sign that read, **Clearance: All Items Five Cents or Ten Cents.** Amazingly, people started buying the stuff that wouldn't sell before. The boss appreciated his enterprising spirit, but more importantly it gave this young clerk an idea: *If everything on these tables sold so fast, why don't I open up a store and call it a Five and Ten Cent Store?*

That man's name was F. W. Woolworth. Going the extra mile for his boss brought him the idea for a multi-billion dollar empire. Five and dime stores are mostly gone in America, but in previous generations Woolworth stores dominated the marketplace and blessed many people.

I served in the Navy for four years; during that time the country experienced a terrible recession. One evening, I went down to Fifth Street in San Diego to a milkshake stand. The unenthusiastic man behind the counter—the owner—was a retired chief petty officer. I ordered a shake and he was back there mumbling and grumbling. He gave me my shake, and it wasn't even a full cup. I said, "Man, you cheated me!"

He said, "Nah, in this economy I can't be giving a full shake. In fact, I've got to raise my prices or I won't make it!" He started complaining about the economy, about his customers, about his vendors, and his suppliers.

There was another little restaurant where I loved to go—a spaghetti house on Fifth Street. I loved the owner, Mr. Bagelli. He would say, "Oh welcome! Welcome to my restaurant! Here, sit here!" I would order a big plate of spaghetti, and it was the best spaghetti I ever ate. Once I noticed my portion seemed bigger. I said, "It looks like I have more spaghetti here."

He replied, "Times are hard for people! I'm giving them a little more spaghetti for their money now." I finished my spaghetti and Mr. Bagelli walked over to the table and said, "You like my spaghetti! I'll get you some more!" I paid once and ate two big portions. He even developed a system where if people needed a meal but couldn't pay, he would let them pay on payday.

Twenty years later I traveled back to San Diego. Everything (including that milkshake shop) that I remembered was gone—except for Mr. Bagelli's restaurant. I discovered that one restaurant had grown into hundreds; he had franchised them all over the western states. A multi-billion dollar company grew out of his concern for his customer and going the extra mile.

Slothful people don't seek work; they try to evade it. The apostle Paul used every opportunity to work to spread the Gospel. His attitude was, "If you become useless, no earthly employer would keep you. Why do you think God would keep you on his payroll if you become worthless and lazy?"

Do you want to move ahead in your ministry, your business, your life? Do you want fruitfulness and multiplication? The key is to be an extra miler. Do more than you have to do. The rewards you receive will be unbelievable.

DEVOTIONAL REFLECTIONS

1: When was the last time you went the extra mile? Explain.

2: Who is someone you admire for going the extra mile? Describe what that person does.

3: How can you go the extra mile today or this week in your leadership? Write down three ideas.

If you don't win the race, you are an average "also-ran," common, mediocre.

The key to success is to make yourself more valuable.

29

CHAPTER

PRACTICING THE EXTRA MILE PRINCIPLE

Back in 1980, I offered *The Art of Pacesetting Leadership* course for the first time and six people signed up. Norm Oberlin was one of them. He worked at General Motors as a general laborer, but he had a dream of getting a management position. He knew he could never get such a position unless he had at least a bachelor's degree, which he did not have at the time.

Norm latched onto this extra mile principle and started applying it at work. He did more than he had to do and made himself more valuable. One day he came into class with a big smile on his face. He had gotten a promotion. They had waived the education qualification for Norm because he was so valuable to the company.

Then God called Norm to the ministry. Our church sent him to a northern vacation destination—Gaylord, Michigan, to be the pastor of a daughter church. Gaylord is surrounded by ski slopes; in winter it is a snowmobiling center. There are 32 good golf courses, not to mention hundreds of inland lakes. But the church was in debt and had virtually no members. The previous pastor had problems and the church dwindled.

Norm and his wife, Barb, dug in and God gave them plenty of opportunities to go the extra mile. The church basement would flood and sewer water would bubble up. Norm and his wife would bail the mess out. Norm told me later that the training he received in *The Art of Pacesetting Leadership* course was more valuable than the college courses he and his wife had taken. He felt he was far ahead of others in training for ministry because the others had received only book knowledge. Pacesetting leadership had given the Oberlins the hands-on, practical aspects of ministry which helped them tremendously.

Under Norm's leadership the church soon grew to 80 people. He went the extra mile in everything. He offered great classes on evangelism. He offered *The Art of Pacesetting Leadership* course and began raising up leaders in the congregation to do the work of the ministry. He watched as people applied the extra mile principle, and many other pacesetting leadership principles, at church, in their businesses, in their homes and in their relationships with the Lord. The effect was transformational. Three of the Oberlin boys went through the Pacesetting Leadership Course and Norm says it is one of the reasons they are in ministry as adults.

Today that church in Gaylord, a town of 5,000, is packed out on Sundays because Norm has taught the people leadership and how to go the extra mile. I visited the church a while ago, and I experienced a vibrant, growing, healthy church.

There will never be a shortage of opportunities for the leader who consistently does more than he or she has to do and strives for quality and excellence in everything. That man or woman will be in demand.

Do you want to win? Prepare better than anyone else. Do you want to prosper? Do more than you have to do. Make yourself more valuable. If you want success in your leadership, go for excellence. Going the extra mile feels so good that you won't want to go back to mediocrity.

BIG REWARDS FOR GOING THE EXTRA MILE

I read a story about a clerk in Pittsburgh who made the decision to treat every woman as if she were his mother, sister, or daughter, and every man as if he were his father, brother, or son. One rainy day an elderly woman with a babushka on her head came into the department store where he worked. She looked like a poor bag lady. All the other clerks said, "Oh, she doesn't have any money!" and turned their backs so they wouldn't have to wait on her. But this young clerk remembered the commitment he had made and thought, "What if she was my mother?" He walked over and said, "Can I help you, ma'am?" She said, "I'm just trying to get out of the rain. I'm waiting for a bus and thought I'd come in here and look around while I wait."

He offered her a chair; she was very appreciative and sat there until her bus came. A couple of months later the department store got a call from Scotland. It was the "bag" lady. She said, "I have a castle I would like to refurbish, and I would like your store to provide the furnishings. I want that nice young man who was so kind to me to coordinate my purchases." The store sent him over to Scotland to find out what she needed. She bought millions of dollars worth of furniture and completely re-furnished her castle. His commission came to what was an enormous amount for the time—something like $4 million dollars in today's money.

The "bag lady" was allegedly Andrew Carnegie's mother.

It reminds me of what the writer to Hebrews said, that we sometimes entertain angels unaware. This lady was no angel, but she certainly blessed that young man! What if he hadn't gone the extra mile to help that woman?

It takes so little to rise above average. It can be just a little more determination than anyone else. You see, the extra mile is a short mile. When Jesus said, "If you have to go one mile, go two," that second one is short compared to all the benefits you receive.

Aim to give a hundred percent, and then go a couple percent more. That extra effort you expend will put you head and shoulders above the average.

DEVOTIONAL REFLECTIONS

1: Have you ever been rewarded for going the extra mile? Tell how.

2: What is one of the toughest tasks you have faced in your leadership? How did you make it a success?

3: Ask the Lord to show you ways you can go the extra mile today.

It takes so little to rise above average. It can be just a little more determination than anyone else.

Just like a toothpaste plant is designed to create toothpaste, churches are designed to create disciples.

30

CHAPTER

TURNING FOLLOWERS INTO LEADERS

This next principle is so powerful and simple that it can advance you years in your business, family and ministry. It is a leadership principle that says leaders must produce other leaders!

The Lord gave Joshua a commission:

Joshua 1:6–7 NLT

[6] "Be strong and courageous, for you are the one who will lead these people to possess all the land I swore to their ancestors I would give them.

[7] Be strong and very courageous. Be careful to obey all the instructions Moses gave you. Do not deviate from them, turning either to the right or to the left. Then you will be successful in everything you do."

A leader is someone who takes people where they otherwise wouldn't go. And a pacesetting leader is someone who doesn't just lead but trains leaders and delegates leadership to others, raising up a new generation of leaders.

Twenty years ago, a young man named Anthony Yeboah from Ghana in West Africa was involved in a satanic cult that worshiped fetishes. Somebody told Anthony about Jesus and he responded to Christ's call.

A missionary pastor saw potential in Anthony and provided him a scholarship to come to Mount Hope Bible Training Institute in Lansing, Michigan. Anthony, who had been rejected by his family for converting to Christ, came to the U.S., took *The Art of Pacesetting Leadership* course and other classes. When his studies were completed we sent him back to West Africa to begin a church on our behalf. Some of our daughter churches in the Mount Hope Church network began supporting him.

Six years later there wasn't a whole lot of progress, but Anthony hung in there. Then suddenly he experienced a breakthrough. Within ten years there were thousands of people attending his churches—including Arabic-speaking Muslims who had turned to Christ. Anthony began meeting with presidents, kings, and world leaders. He is a humble unassuming man—you would never know the success God has given him by looking at him. The reports I heard were so amazing that I sent a team over to verify the fruit. It was all true.

I love what Anthony told me about pacesetting leadership, "I read it over and over and over. I got hold of the principles and put them into practice. It gave me the vision of how to do it. It helped me to see what God has done in Lansing, and I believed I could go even higher than that. Pacesetting leadership has been in most of what we have used. It has helped me to be a good leader and has been a great help to businessmen and small businessmen to use those principles with workers and that sort of thing."

Anthony started orphanages, and is teaching business principles and pacesetting leadership to people all over Africa. He tells me that in the 316 churches he established, there are at least 60,000 members. He has conducted crusades with evangelists such as Reinhard Bonnke, Richard Roberts, and T.L. Osborn. Anthony's ministry has been credited with more than 11,000,000 people who have made decisions for Christ. Recently he brought the president of Burundi to Michigan to speak at a conference. He has worked with the presidents of Nigeria, Burundi, and Ethiopia, to build orphanages and schools in their countries.

Anthony could not have done all this on his own. He learned the principles of pacesetting leadership and then trained and delegated leaders for the sake of multiplying and filling the earth with followers of Christ.

BUILD THE PEOPLE

The principle of building people up and staying focused on your vision applies to all areas of life, but let's look specifically at how this applies to ministry.

What is the main goal of a church? To go out and teach all nations. That is the Great Commission Jesus gave to us, and no one is excluded from it.[1] Every believer has the common mission to go into all the world and teach the Good News of Jesus Christ. So a church must produce disciples. If it doesn't, it can hardly be called a church.

For example, say there was a toothpaste company and one day the CEO visited the factory and saw doughnuts and jelly-filled rolls coming off the conveyor belts; he would know immediately there was a problem. Money had been invested to make toothpaste, but instead the factory was producing doughnuts. The workers might say, "Doughnuts improve the morale around here. We love taking a break and having doughnuts. So we're making those instead of toothpaste."

You would no longer call that a toothpaste factory; you would call it a doughnut factory. The same is true for the church. In

---

[1] Matthew 28:18–20

a church, money is invested in the form of tithes and offerings. Man-hours go in. What is the church supposed to be producing? Disciples! Jesus' mandate was to train people to do what he did and then let them do it. If a church is producing only converts, it's not a church. Conversion is only part of the process. The ultimate goal is to make disciples.

The same principle applies to businesses and families and organizations of all kinds. If you have strayed from your foundational purpose, then the nature of what you do has changed. Ask yourself, are you leading people toward the original goal or to a different destination? Is it time to get back on track?

The first day I became pastor, Mary Jo and I took our kids to The Regal 8 Motel—just eight dollars a night. The kids slept in the dresser drawers. We wanted to pray and seek the Lord for the future of our church. The Lord spoke to me and said, "David, if you will build the people, I will build the church."

I started building people. It began with six disciples in my office every Tuesday, training them to do the work of the ministry. It grew into the entire Mount Hope Bible Training Institute that, to date, has produced 276 full-time ministers. Not only were we winning people to the Lord, we were training them in his ways.

Once I had a vision of a man who was full of holes. He was missing an arm and leg and other parts. I asked, "Lord, what is that?" He answered, "That is you in the ministry I gave you. You are not complete in yourself. The body of Christ is not complete unless everybody fits in and finds their ministry and gifts. You have missing parts. To make the ministry complete, educate, impart, and delegate to people. Then it becomes a whole body."

That was an important moment as I realized that a pacesetting leader is supposed to lead others into their calling so the local body, business, or endeavor will be complete. Moses, one of the greatest leaders in history, had to learn this same lesson.

Exodus 18:13 NLT
The next day, Moses took his seat to hear the people's disputes against each other. They waited before him from morning till evening.

"Pastor Moses" was leading two million people. Everybody wanted to see him personally. They stood in line to have him counsel them. Moses thought he was being a good pastor by handling every question and dispute and being all things to all people. Some people run a business or an enterprise the same way, not realizing that when you have your hands in everything, your bottom line will be nothing. Here is the lesson Moses learned from his father-in-law:

Exodus 18:14 NLT
[14] When Moses' father-in-law saw all that Moses was doing for the people, he asked, "What are you really accomplishing here? Why are you trying to do all this alone while everyone stands around you from morning till evening?"
[15] Moses said to his father-in-law, Because the people come to me to inquire of God.
[16] When they have a dispute they come to me, and I judge between a man and his neighbor, and I make them know the statutes of God and His laws.
[17] Moses' father-in-law said to him, The thing that you are doing is not good.
[18] You will surely wear out both yourself and this people with you, for the thing is too heavy for you; you are not able to perform it all by yourself.
[19] Listen now to [me]; I will counsel you, and God will be with you. You shall represent the people before God, bringing their cases and causes to Him,
[20] Teaching them the decrees and laws, showing them the way they must walk and the work they must do.
[21] Moreover, you shall choose able men from all the people—God-fearing men of truth who hate unjust gain—and place them over thousands, hundreds, fifties, and tens, to be their rulers.

[22] And let them judge the people at all times; every great matter they shall bring to you, but every small matter they shall judge. So it will be easier for you, and they will bear the burden with you.

[23] If you will do this, and God so commands you, you will be able to endure [the strain], and all these people also will go to their [tents] in peace.

[24] So Moses listened to and heeded the voice of his father-in-law and did all that he had said.

WHAT WAS THE FRUIT OF THAT DECISION?

1: Moses did not have a nervous breakdown but was able to continue leading the people for forty years.

He went from being on the verge of collapse and saying, "God, if you're going to treat me like this, just kill me—I'd rather be dead!" to becoming a pacesetting leader over the long term.[2]

2: All the people's needs were met!

3: Others got to exercise their gifts and grow in their own leadership skills.

For every person you train as a leader, and who goes on to serve the church, it will grow by twelve to fifteen people. I'm not even sure how it happens or why, but I have seen that pattern for years. People who get involved and are trained in leadership are engines of growth for your church. I believe this principle applies to your business as well. That is how the Mount Hope network of churches has grown and is now approaching 100,000 members. It all goes back to training people to be disciples and delegating the work to them.

This is exactly the example Jesus set when he trained his disciples. First he sent the twelve, then another seventy, then all who believe. Jesus really loved training his disciples. After the crowds

---

[2] Numbers 11:14

The way to sustain growth is to make disciples.

went away, he seemed eager to get alone with them to teach them how to be effective leaders. Why? Because he knew these men would carry on his work after he ascended to heaven.

We should have the same passion to train leaders to run with our vision.

UNLIMITED GROWTH

Many leaders try to build their church or enterprise like a triangle with the tip of the triangle pointing down and the whole weight of the business, company, or ministry on one key person —the leader. As the undertaking grows, the pressure on the leader also grows, and that leads to rapid "burn-out."

The way to get unlimited growth without overwhelming pressure is to make disciples. Then the growth is shared among everyone.

Remember that you cannot possibly accomplish all the functions needed in a church, business, small group, or classroom you lead. If you don't train up leaders, you will severely limit the size and success of your undertaking.

I quickly found out that I'm not good at many things that need to happen in a church. For example, I am a terrible counselor. I had a habit of telling people, "Get out of your sin and everything will be okay." I offended more people than I helped. Once, a woman came to me and said, "I'm confused!"

I replied, "Then there's sin in your life. The Bible says in James 3:16, 'For where envy and self-seeking exist, confusion and every evil thing are there,' so you must be entertaining evil."

She stormed out and I thought she would never come back. The next week she came by the church and she seemed happy and content. She said, "Pastor, I was really mad at you last week when you told me that. But I got to praying, and you were right. I made my boyfriend move out this week." I think that was the only time my efforts at counseling worked.

I'm also not much of a comforter. One man called the church and demanded that I come see him in the hospital and not send "some second-rate person" instead. I went to the hospital, found his room, laid hands on him and prayed for him. He died! Things may have turned out better if I had sent the healing team instead!

The fact is, if your church or business is going to grow, you've got to train others and delegate work to them. Back in the 1960s, when Chuck Smith of Calvary Chapel in Costa Mesa, California, had twenty-five people in his church it wasn't growing because the people didn't want to do the work. "That's what we pay the pastor to do," was their attitude. So he started equipping young "hippies" to be leaders and then the church grew to 35,000.

Training and delegating others will cause multiplication in every area of your life and cause your business, your ministry, or your church to fill the earth. The entire world would be filled with the glory of God in a tangible way in just a few years if every believer would make disciples.

As pacesetting leaders, let's make more pacesetting leaders!

DEVOTIONAL REFLECTIONS

1: Are you intentionally raising up leaders under you?
Who are they?

2: Are you afraid to give up control by delegating?
Explain why.

3: Now pray for God to give you the heart to train other
leaders and delegate responsibility to them. What can you
do this week to start down that path?

Authority is real, rebellion is real—and divine discipline is real.

31
CHAPTER

DIVINE DISCIPLINE

I had a sobering experience early in my ministry. At that time, I hosted a Bible study with twenty-four people in my home. We had a coffee can with a hole in the top, and the Bible study members would contribute a dollar or two. When we got to $250 we would buy tracts to hand out to help get people saved and begin to disciple them.

One man who attended the Bible study was very disruptive. He would say outrageous things, lie about people, and disrupt discussions. One night after the meeting, I checked how much was in the can and all the money was gone. I knew there had been at least two hundred dollars in there. I was furious. I just *knew* it was this man who had taken the money.

That night I prayed an amateur's prayer, "God, I don't know exactly how to do this, but I read that Paul delivered a man living in sin over to Satan."

1 Corinthians 5:5 NLT
Then you must throw this man out and hand him over to Satan so that his sinful nature will be destroyed and he himself will be saved on the day the Lord returns.

The redemptive result would save their spirit. I continued, "I pray that whoever stole this money be turned over to Satan for the destruction of his flesh, that he might learn not to sin." It was a scary thing to do, and I haven't done it more than two times in the past forty years. The next day I got a call.

"Brother Dave," the voice said, Joe (not his real name) is in the hospital and wants you to go see him." The man in the hospital was the one I thought took the money. He had experienced a heart attack the night I prayed! When I went into his room, he was crying and repenting. He told me he took the money and was sorry for all the lies he had told. He asked me to pray for him. I did and God healed him. He became a wonderful, honest, humble person after that and actually brought many people to church.

This is one of the most frightening and misunderstood topics in our study of leadership: authority, rebellion, and divine discipline.

Romans 11:22 NKJV
Therefore consider the goodness and severity of God: on those who fell, severity; but toward you, goodness, if you continue in His goodness. Otherwise you also will be cut off.

Authority is real, rebellion is real—and divine discipline is real. As a leader you must understand how to deal with them.

THE REALITY OF REBELLION

St. Paul told the church in Corinth to, "deliver such a one to Satan for the destruction of the flesh, that his spirit may be saved in the day of the Lord Jesus." In essence, Paul told the church, "There is a man in your church who is committing such a detestable sin, he must be turned over to Satan to be destroyed so that his spirit might be saved."[1]

---

[1] 1 Corinthians 5:5

Paul also wrote to his young "son" in the faith, Timothy, about another instance of discipline.

1 Timothy 1:18–20 NKJV

[18] This charge I commit to you, son Timothy, according to the prophecies previously made concerning you, that by them you may wage the good warfare,

[19] having faith and a good conscience, which some having rejected, concerning the faith have suffered shipwreck,

[20] of whom are Hymenaeus and Alexander, whom I delivered to Satan that they may learn not to blaspheme.

The redemptive result: that they might learn not to blaspheme and would come to repentance.

Does God allow Satan to bring serious complications into the lives of people who hinder a leader who is operating in God's will? Does God allow people to experience serious problems, or even die before their time, to prevent a hindrance to his plans? My experience says yes.

Pastor John O'Connor, my friend, established thirteen churches in the Michigan area and God seemed to use him in the healing ministry. People were healed of cancer and of many other illnesses. But one woman in the church kept antagonizing him and telling lies about him. One day John got a call. This woman was on the line and she said, "My son is in the hospital. They don't expect him to live. Would you please come and pray for him?"

John, being a man of compassion, went to the hospital and found her son's room. The boy lay in the bed with tubes coming in and going out of him. His neck was in some kind of a brace. No one was around, so John laid hands on the boy and began to pray for his healing.

Just then his mother jumped out from behind a curtain and started screaming, "He's choking my son! He's choking my son!" She ran to the nurse's station screeching, "There's a man in there choking my son!"

John was shocked and embarrassed. It's amazing how Satan tries to discredit genuine leadership. He went home that night and prayed, "God, you've got to do something about that woman. She's plotting to destroy my reputation." Not long after that, a storm moved through town. Two men who lived near that woman were sitting on their front porch the night it happened. They testified to what they saw. A lightning bolt came out of the sky, turned sharply, and entered the home where this woman lived. That lightening bolt struck her. Some people survive lightning strikes, but she did not.

Was that a coincidence? Or did she go one step too far against God's authority?

MORE POWERFUL THAN THE LAW

Of all the sins that people commit, it seems like the most severe sin in God's eyes is when someone hinders a leader whom God has appointed.

I was a young preacher, thirty-six years old, and having severe heart pains. My chest was in pain for eighteen months because of the stress caused by rebels within the church. I didn't know how to deal with their rebellion and I told nobody but Mary Jo, my wife, about these chest pains. One day Jim, a missionary, called me and said, "Dave, I'm in Grand Rapids. I want to bring somebody over to meet you." It was a Wednesday and I thought, *I don't have time. I'm preparing for Wednesday night service*, but I agreed to meet them anyway.

Jim came into my office with a woman named Lois. Lois seemed strange. She was jibber-jabbering away and sounded like a nut case. My first impression was that she was absolutely kooky.

Suddenly, she jumped out of her chair, ran around my desk, swung my swivel chair around and threw her arms around me! I was ready to scream for help. She put her hands on my chest and started making faith commands. She didn't know about my heart pains. Jim didn't know. Nobody else but Mary Jo knew, but God knew. The pains had grown increasingly intense, and I couldn't forget that my dad had died when he was only forty years old of heart trouble. She prayed and spoke to my arteries and talked to my heart. After that strange encounter, she left and the intense heart pains went away entirely.

I learned that Lois was a Catholic evangelist from Oklahoma, and God had told her there was a pastor in Michigan who needed prayer. She immediately bought a ticket to the cheapest place she could fly into, which was Grand Rapids. She called Jim because God said, "Jim will know who it is," and it turned out I was the recipient of God's wonderful grace that day.

I heard more of Lois' story later. She had been holding charismatic Bible studies in her Catholic church, and it was growing rapidly. People were being born again, filled with the Holy Spirit and healed of their diseases. But there was a judge in that church who didn't approve of her ministry one bit.

One night, Lois prayed for a woman who fell down ostensibly under the power of the "Holy Spirit" and began screaming, "My back! My back!" She sued Lois, claiming her fall hurt her back. Even though there was no measurable medical evidence that this woman sustained a back injury, Lois and her husband had to sell their home to pay the attorney. The judge presiding over the case was the church member who didn't approve of the charismatic things going on. He ruled against Lois. She and her husband lost all their property. However, what happened next is interesting.

I was told that one week later the judge's son committed suicide. The judge was so devastated by his son's death that he had to be committed into a mental institution—all within just thirty days of pronouncing his judgment against Lois and her husband. Was it a coincidence, or the judgment of God and divine discipline at work?

THE NEVADA SCAM

My friend, Reverend Ivar Frick, was going to minister in Nevada. As he drove along a lonely, empty stretch of desert road, he was pulled over by a small-town sheriff and given an unfair speeding ticket. He walked into the Justice of the Peace's office to protest. The place was a cluttered mess. A man came out of the back holding a can of beer and said, "That'll be $150."

Reverend Frick stated, "I was not exceeding the speed limit. This whole thing is a setup."

The Justice sneered, "I don't care!"

Brother Frick said, "I'm a man of God. I'm on my way to minister. How can you do this to a man of God?"

He responded, "I don't give a blankety-blank who you are. It's $150 or jail!"

Reverend Frick paid the $150 and went on to the town where he was ministering. He ministered that night and the next day. In his hotel room, he picked up a newspaper. The Justice of the Peace he had just encountered was found shot to death. The mob had come through and he had tried to give them an unfair ticket, but they literally didn't put up with it.

Coincidence, or did he go one step too far and come under the severity of God?

TWO POWERS

Every time a person criticizes a leader appointed by God, especially in the church, it's like saying, "Jesus, your bride is ugly." How many men would put up with somebody saying, "Your bride is ugly"? They would come under your severity rather than your goodness.

Most people don't realize there are only two powers at work in the world: the authority of God, and satanic rebellion. Everyone is operating under one of those two powers at any given time.

HIDDEN PRINCIPLE OF REBELLION

2 Thessalonians 2:7 NLT
For this lawlessness is already at work secretly, and it will remain secret until the one who is holding it back steps out of the way.

Rebellion is always hidden, covert, occult. Occult means: secret, mysterious, or hidden. Satanic rebellion produces no fruit or bad fruit. Under God's authority, there is order and organization, just as there is in all of creation. People in satanic rebellion choose to live in confusion, disorder, and division. Under God's authority, we follow God's will; with satanic rebellion, people become mavericks. Even Christians can behave this way, for example saying, "I don't need a pastor; it's me and Jesus! I don't need to go to church. I can have church wherever I want."

A woman came to my Bible study years ago. She was married and had an eight-year-old son. Her husband wasn't a Christian. The Scriptures say that if your husband is not saved, by your good works and beautiful spirit you will be able to lead him to the Lord. But she was more of the,"I want to do something for God all by myself" type without acknowledging spiritual authority.

One night she came to the Bible study and said, "God has called me to be a missionary to Mexico." She stomped her foot and said, "I'm going to Mexico to obey God and be a missionary even if I have to get rid of my husband!" Imagine the example that set for an eight-year-old boy: "We're going to get rid of daddy so we can go to Mexico and be missionaries for Jesus."

She went to Mexico based on her "faith," but if you don't understand and operate under authority, it's not real faith. She declared, "God will supply all my needs! I'm going to work for Jesus." She left her husband and took her son to Mexico to be a missionary. In less than three months she was broke and living with a man in San Antonio, Texas, who wasn't her husband.

Is it any wonder kids turn out the way they do? The seeds of rebellion blossom into all sorts of wickedness.

The truth is, Satan does not care if someone who is not sent by God preaches the Word or tries to lead others. He knows they will only make a mess of things when they don't have the power of God behind them. The reason the members of the early church had power to do miracles was because they were acting with God's "sent" authority. If God does not send you, if you just "went" because of your own ideas, you will get into trouble.

Acts 19: 11–16 NLT

[11] God gave Paul the power to perform unusual miracles.

[12] When handkerchiefs or aprons that had merely touched his skin were placed on sick people, they were healed of their diseases, and evil spirits were expelled.

[13] A group of Jews was traveling from town to town casting out evil spirits. They tried to use the name of the Lord Jesus in their incantation, saying, "I command you in the name of Jesus, whom Paul preaches, to come out!"

[14] Seven sons of Sceva, a leading priest, were doing this.

[15] But one time when they tried it, the evil spirit replied, "I know Jesus, and I know Paul, but who are you?"

[16] Then the man with the evil spirit leaped on them, overpowered them, and attacked them with such violence that they fled from the house, naked and battered.

This man possessed of a demon turned on these sons of Sceva, insulted them, and beat them so badly they fled naked. Talk about "went" leadership!

If a private puts on a general's uniform, he might strut around the military base for a while and get some people to salute him, but he will have no real authority and soon he will be court-martialed for impersonating an officer.

True ministry is always "sent" ministry. Jesus said, "So pray to the Lord who is in charge of the harvest; ask him to send more workers into his fields."[2] Even Jesus, himself, was "sent."

John 3:17 NLT
God sent his Son into the world not to judge the world, but to save the world through him.

It's a dangerous thing to send yourself and go by our own presumption and not God's leading and blessing. And it's dangerous for people to resist God's established leaders. We'll learn more about that in the next chapter.

DEVOTIONAL REFLECTIONS

1: **Have you ever encountered rebellion? How did you handle it?**

2: **Have you ever exercised divine discipline? What was the circumstance?**

---

[2] Matthew 9:38 NLT

No leader is perfect, but you want one who is sent by God

32
CHAPTER

SENT VS. WENT LEADERS

Mary Jo went to Bible school with a beautiful couple named Aaron and Carrie. They were a called to be missionaries to Mexico, but they weren't going to go unless their church sent them. Their church was small and was meeting in a garage.

Aaron and Carrie started serving the pastor and church faithfully. It can be difficult when you have a call that hasn't manifested yet, but they waited patiently. One day, the pastor came to them and said, "I know we're a small church, but we really need to start a missions ministry. We'd like you to be the first missionaries and we will send you to Mexico." The church bought them a brand-new diesel truck, they went to Mexico and enjoyed a successful and fruitful ministry.

What a difference between them and the woman who went with her son on her own initiative. The couple was sent; she just went.

STRUCK BLIND

Acts 13:1–3 NLT
[1] Among the prophets and teachers of the church at Antioch of Syria were Barnabas, Simeon (called "the black man"),

Lucius (from Cyrene), Manaen (the childhood companion of King Herod Antipas, and Saul.
² One day as these men were worshiping the Lord and fasting, the Holy Spirit said, "Dedicate Barnabas and Saul for the special work to which I have called them."
³ So after more fasting and prayer, the men laid their hands on them and sent them on their way.)

I like what we learn here: the Holy Spirit had already called Saul and Barnabas, but now was letting the church know. I wonder how long the call was there and Paul and Barnabas were waiting for the church to see it! Talk about patience!

Notice that the Holy Spirit did not send them until it was recognized by a church that was fasting and praying and willing to send them.

When you are sent under the authority of God, you have the authority of God. The account continues:

Acts 13:6–11 NLT
⁶ Afterward they traveled from town to town across the entire island until finally they reached Paphos, where they met a Jewish sorcerer, a false prophet named Bar-Jesus.
⁷ He had attached himself to the governor, Sergius Paulus, who was an intelligent man. The governor invited Barnabas and Saul to visit him, for he wanted to hear the word of God.
⁸ But Elymas, the sorcerer (as his name means in Greek), interfered and urged the governor to pay no attention to what Barnabas and Saul said. He was trying to keep the governor from believing.
⁹ Saul, also known as Paul, was filled with the Holy Spirit, and he looked the sorcerer in the eye.
¹⁰ Then he said, "You son of the devil, full of every sort of deceit and fraud, and enemy of all that is good! Will you never stop perverting the true ways of the Lord?
¹¹ Watch now, for the Lord has laid his hand of punishment upon you, and you will be struck blind. You will not see the sunlight for some time." Instantly mist and darkness came

over the man's eyes, and he began groping around begging for someone to take his hand and lead him.

Paul was filled with righteous wrath. The Holy Spirit influenced him to light into this man, Elymas, who was "full of all subtilty," as the *King James Version* puts it, which is how poison works. Most of the time you don't know poison is there until it has worked its deadly effect. Interestingly, this man was a Jew. He was supposed to be a son of Abraham, but he was a "went," not a "sent." Paul said he was "full of mischief" which means recklessness, not understanding authority, maligning the authority of God. Paul said, "...thou child of the devil, thou enemy of all righteousness, wilt thou not cease to pervert the right ways of the Lord?"

With his authority, Paul pronounced judgment on this rebellious man. Sent and influenced by the Holy Spirit, Paul brought divine discipline on rebellious Elymas the sorcerer.

As always with divine discipline, there was a redemptive result.

Acts 13:2 NLT
When the governor saw what had happened, he became a believer, for he was astonished at the teaching about the Lord.

GOD'S PATTERN OF DISCIPLINE

God moves in divine discipline throughout the Scriptures when someone rebels against or chips away at God's leadership. When Adam rebelled he lost his wealth, abundance, and luxury. Noah's son Ham pointed out his father's nakedness, and Noah pronounced a curse on him. Ham's descendants were wiped off the face of the earth while the other two brothers, who had honored their father, received a pronouncement of blessing.

Miriam rebelled against Moses and leprosy struck her. Dathan and Abiram followed Korah, leaders who were rebelling against Moses. Something happened that had never happened before—the world's very first earthquake. At the homes of Dathan,

Abiram, and all those who rebelled against Moses the earth opened up and swallowed them alive. They lost everything in a moment because of rebellion.

I've seen examples of this time and again in the present day. There was a young minister in Michigan who was full of the Spirit of God and wanted to do great things for God. Three board members opposed him and ripped him to shreds. A week later those three board members were out taking a joyride in an airplane, something went wrong, and it crashed. All three of them were killed. Coincidence, or the judgment of God?

There was a young, gifted evangelist who was a great musician and preacher. People were getting saved under his ministry, but somehow he became deluded in his thinking and grew very arrogant. He rented the Mabee Center at Oral Roberts University to hold a meeting, and in that meeting he tore apart Oral Roberts and Oral Roberts University—right on their own property! Within days, he was killed.

No leader is perfect; that's not my point. But it is a dangerous thing to go after God's established leaders. We may disagree with other people, but we don't have to tear them to shreds in a rebellious, unloving, public way.

Some years ago, there was a move in Congress to shut down television ministries. Rex Humbard told me this story over lunch. Rex testified during the congressional hearings. After the questioning concluded, an aide pointed to Rex and said, "I'm going to get all you preachers off the air!"

Rex stood up and said, "Mister, you're forgetting one thing—God." That afternoon, the man went to the dentist for a simple procedure. When the dentist gave him a shot of Novocaine he had a severe reaction and died in the dental chair. That ended the witch hunt of Christian television preachers.

Were these events just coincidence, or did they suffer the severity of God's judgment? I can't answer that with certainty, but I've determined to be gracious and non-judgemental toward all men and women of God, regardless of their perceived flaws and weaknesses.

Oral Roberts Ministries was just taking off and his headquarters was going to be in Enid, Oklahoma. He was having a big crusade there when three men came to him one night and said, "Reverend Roberts, we know that the anointing is on you, and we want to be in on the money end."

Oral replied, "Gentlemen, God told me, 'Never touch the gold and never touch the glory.'"

They said, "If you don't let us in on the financial end of your ministry, we're going to destroy you." Still, Oral refused.

His huge crusades started dwindling in size. Suddenly there was a cloud of suspicion over Oral's ministry. He didn't know what had happened. People he once loved now seemed to avoid him. Then Oral learned that those three men were spreading doubt about his ministry.

He had to leave Enid and move to Tulsa. Six months later he was holding a crusade. A wobbling, emaciated man came through the healing line and in a whimpering voice asked, "Brother Roberts, can you please forgive me?" Oral recognized who this man was—one of the three men who had wanted in on the financial end of God's business.

Oral said, "Of course I forgive you." Oral laid hands on that man and he was healed. The other two men had died within six months of opposing Oral. The man who repented became a humble servant of Christ and a regent at Oral Roberts University for many years. Thank God for the redemptive results of divine discipline!

Proverbs 6:14–19 KJV (emphasis added)
14 Frowardness is in his heart, he deviseth mischief continually; he soweth discord.

THE RESULT

¹⁵ Therefore shall his calamity come suddenly; suddenly shall he be broken without remedy.

¹⁶ *These six things doth the Lord hate: yea, seven are an abomination unto him:*

¹⁷ A *proud look,* a *lying tongue,* and *hands that shed innocent blood,*

¹⁸ An heart that deviseth *wicked imaginations,* feet that be *swift in running to mischief,*

¹⁹ A *false witness* that speaketh lies, and he that *soweth discord* among brethren.

All these examples should be a warning: Watch that you don't come too strongly against people who are sent by God. The most famous people in Christian history were accused of being heretics, from Smith Wigglesworth to Charles Finney; Billy Sunday to D. L. Moody. Don't tear down a man's reputation because God often gives people a lot of space to repent and make it right. I've known men who taught false doctrines, and even belonged to cults, and repented. God is much more patient than we are. But he can also be surprisingly swift in bringing divine discipline when he wills it.

Let me finish this chapter with this story to show how we all get used in our own way by God. I found it in my notes from the 1970s and am not sure who wrote it first.

Parable of the Carpenter's Tools

Mr. Hammer was presiding at the meeting of the tools. Brother Screwdriver complained, "Brother Hammer's got to go! He's always making noise, always knocking." Hammer responded, "I think Brother Screwdriver should go because he has to be turned around all the time to get him to do his job." Someone else said, "Brother Plane has to go. He's always wants to touch the surface. He never goes deep." Brother Plane piped up, "I think Brother

Sandpaper ought to go because he's always rubbing people the wrong way." Sandpaper spoke up and said, "Then Brother Saw must go 'cause he's always cutting things up and leaving sawdust all over the place."

Then the Carpenter from Nazareth came in and said, "I need all of you. We have a job for each of you to do. Put yourselves in my hands. Let me use you." So when each gave himself to the Carpenter, together they built a church for preaching the Gospel, a bridge for understanding, a house for a poor Christian family. This is what happens when the tools are put in the Carpenter's hands and are all used for the purpose for which they were made.

Authority is real. Rebellion is real. Divine discipline is real. Be a "sent" leader, not just a "went" leader, and let the Lord deal with those who oppose his work. If you are in his will, he will protect and promote you and provide everything you need.

DEVOTIONAL REFLECTIONS

1: Tell of a time you waited for the right time to be "sent."

2: Have you ever "went" on your own, outside of God's timing and blessing?

3: Ask God to make you "sent" not "went" in all you do and to respect his authority in all areas of life.

When a leader falls, it's not just that leader and his family who are destroyed.

33

LEAVING A LEGACY

Leadership is about influence over the long term. You want to leave a legacy. A year after you're gone, and people are sitting around the Thanksgiving table talking about you what do you want them to say?

"He did a lot of good things for a while, but he sure messed up in the end!" Or, "She had a real impact on my life, and she stayed on track all the way. What an outstanding example of leadership."

Of course you want to leave a lasting legacy. In America today, there seems to be a leadership crisis. People call themselves leaders, but they really are not. They may be managers, or they may have a position or a title, but they're not leading from the heart. Genuine leaders have strong character. If you have exceptional leadership skills but weak character, you're a charlatan.

Jesus called such people "false prophets," because though they were exceptional in what they did, their characters were shabby.[1] Some were anointed and some were appointed, but somewhere along life's journey they failed in matters of character. When they

---

[1] Matthew 7 and 24

compromised their character, or they failed to develop extraordinary skills, they ended up on the scrap heap of life.

A POWERFUL VISUAL

I grew up in Jackson, Michigan, where a man named Sam Glick had a scrap yard. Old cars would come into the scrap yard by the truckload. Mr. Glick had a machine that would crush them into tiny square lumps of steel. An electromagnet would grab them up and load them onto a train to be taken and melted down.

An automobile is made for a purpose. It's not made to be wrecked. People's lives are made for a purpose, but think of all the lives that have landed on the scrap heap when they were not meant to be there. I don't want it to be you, or the people you lead, ending up on the garbage pile.

There's a verse in the Gospels that haunts me.

John 6:66 NLT
At this point many of his disciples turned away and deserted him.

I often wonder how many who came to Christ, and even ministered alongside Christ, walked away from him.

Jesus not only attracts people; he sifts them. I remember a minister who bragged about going into nightclubs and witnessing. It was really just an excuse to hang out in nightclubs. "That's where my church is," he said. "I preach the Gospel there." Then another evangelist spotted him on an airplane with a woman who wasn't his wife. He was sitting there sipping whiskey. The evangelist went over and said, "If you repent, I won't tell your wife. But if you don't repent, she has to know." The man who preached in nightclubs said, "God understands. I have special needs that other men don't have." I can almost hear the crunch of that scrap machine turning the wreckage of his ministry into a tiny metal cube.

I served as a regent at a Christian universiy, and we had a terrific minister who was exciting and had great ministry skills. Then we started hearing rumors about his lack of character. Sure enough, we discovered that he and his secretary were having certain "meetings," and we had to dismiss him. The next thing you know he was on cable television appearing in a comedy club saying, "Yeah, I used to be a preacher of the Gospel." Everybody laughed as he ripped apart faith in Christ. It all started with a bad "thistle seed" that got planted in his garden and grew into a character lapse, and that led to losing the glory God had planned for his life.

When a leader falls, it's not just that leader and his family who are destroyed. It's more like a nuclear explosion. There is the original damage of the explosion, but the worst part is the "radioactive" contamination that affects people's lives for years to come.

The Bible gives encouragement that you can complete this journey as a pacesetting leader.

Hebrews 12:1-17 MSG

[1-3] Do you see what this means—all these pioneers who blazed the way, all these veterans cheering us on? It means we'd better get on with it. Strip down, start running—and never quit! No extra spiritual fat, no parasitic sins. Keep your eyes on Jesus, who both began and finished this race we're in. Study how he did it. Because he never lost sight of where he was headed—that exhilarating finish in and with God— he could put up with anything along the way: Cross, shame, whatever. And now he's there, in the place of honor, right alongside God. When you find yourselves flagging in your faith, go over that story again, item by item, that long litany of hostility he plowed through. That will shoot adrenaline into your souls!

[4-11] In this all-out match against sin, others have suffered far worse than you, to say nothing of what Jesus went through—all that bloodshed! So don't feel sorry for your-

selves. Or have you forgotten how good parents treat children, and that God regards you as his children?

My dear child, don't shrug off God's discipline,
    but don't be crushed by it either.
It's the child he loves that he disciplines;
    the child he embraces, he also corrects.

God is educating you; that's why you must never drop out. He's treating you as dear children. This trouble you're in isn't punishment; it's training, the normal experience of children. Only irresponsible parents leave children to fend for themselves. Would you prefer an irresponsible God? We respect our own parents for training and not spoiling us, so why not embrace God's training so we can truly live? While we were children, our parents did what seemed best to them. But God is doing what is best for us, training us to live God's holy best. At the time, discipline isn't much fun. It always feels like it's going against the grain. Later, of course, it pays off handsomely, for it's the well-trained who find themselves mature in their relationship with God.

[12–13] So don't sit around on your hands! No more dragging your feet! Clear the path for long-distance runners so no one will trip and fall, so no one will step in a hole and sprain an ankle. Help each other out. And run for it!

[14–17] Work at getting along with each other and with God. Otherwise you'll never get so much as a glimpse of God. Make sure no one gets left out of God's generosity. Keep a sharp eye out for weeds of bitter discontent. A thistle or two gone to seed can ruin a whole garden in no time. Watch out for the Esau syndrome: trading away God's lifelong gift in order to satisfy a short-term appetite. You well know how Esau later regretted that impulsive act and wanted God's blessing—but by then it was too late, tears or no tears.

Determine not to land on Glick's scrap heap. Satan respects no neutral zones. He hates Jesus Christ, and you represent Jesus Christ, so he will target you. Paul said it will be a fight to the end.

1 Timothy 6:12 NLT
Fight the good fight for the true faith. Hold tightly to the eternal life to which God has called you, which you have confessed so well before many witnesses.

Fight for your legacy and keep a watchful eye out for traps. In the next chapters, I will spell out some of the major pitfalls in the pacesetter's path.

DEVOTIONAL REFLECTIONS

1: **Have you seen people end up on the scrap heap of life? Explain what happened.**

2: **Write down what you hope people say about you after you go to be with the Lord.**

3: **Ask God to prepare your legacy even now, so that you can walk the pacesetter's path with confidence.**

Beware of pride.

34

CHAPTER

PITFALLS IN THE PACESETTER'S PATH

Let's take a look at some of the major pitfalls on the pacesetter's path—so we can avoid them all.

1: An off-centered life

A healthy Christian life is Christ-centered. Not me-centered, not ministry-centered, not business-centered, and not family-centered. The only pleasing life to God is Christ-centered. You cannot be Christ-centered and ministry-centered. You cannot be Christ-centered and leadership-centered. Some men and women get so caught up in their leadership position they neglect to keep Christ at the very center. Jesus said...

Matthew 6:24 NKJV
"No one can serve two masters; for either he will hate the one and love the other, or else he will be loyal to the one and despise the other. You cannot serve God and mammon."

That applies to everything in life. You can't serve God and something else. Stay centered!

2: Neglecting prayer and study of God's Word

This is probably one of the most common areas where leaders stray from the pacesetter's path. The pacesetter's life must be saturated with prayer and meditation on God's Word.

I met a group of pastors at a breakfast, and we were talking about prayer. One pastor said, "I don't have time for prayer anymore. My people have so many needs, they call me the first thing in the morning and they keep calling me until late at night. I have to be there for them." I didn't say anything to him but I thought, *you're heading for a fall.* He had left the pacesetter's path.

Not long after that, he went to counsel a woman at her house. He ended up spending the night, and it destroyed his ministry and his family.

Psalm 1:1–3 MSG
[1] How well God must like you—you don't hang out at Sin Saloon, you don't slink along Dead-End Road, you don't go to Smart-Mouth College.
[2-3] Instead you thrill to God's Word, you chew on Scripture day and night.
You're a tree replanted in Eden, bearing fresh fruit every month,
Never dropping a leaf, always in blossom.

My prayer for you is that you will bear fruit every month.

Joshua 1:8–9 NLT
[8] "Study this Book of Instruction continually. Meditate on it day and night so you will be sure to obey everything written in it. Only then will you prosper and succeed in all you do.
[9] This is my command—be strong and courageous! Do not be afraid or discouraged. For the Lord your God is with you wherever you go."

When I met the woman who was to become my wife, her face shone like an angel. She had a radiance about her, and I didn't know what it was. I learned later that she was a prayer warrior! She would go over to the golf course and find a place in the woods. There she would worship God. She was like Moses when he had been in the presence of God. His face would shine so brightly that he had to put a veil over it.

I am grateful that Mary Jo became my wife because her face still shines. She still seeks the Lord every day. She's the kind who can pray four hours and still say, "I just haven't prayed enough!" What an inspiration to me.

Don't wander away from prayer and meditating on God's Word. It will guard your life and give you a strong foundation to your leadership.

3: Lack of focus

We had a saying around our church: "Winners focus; losers spray." You can't keep adding things to your life without eliminating some other things. Every so often you have to take an inventory of your commitments and say, "What is my primary focus? What commitments need to stop?" I like people to have only one major ministry instead of spreading themselves too thin.

If you find yourself stressed out or lacking excitement for your task, it may be that you have taken on too many things in your enthusiasm to grow and serve. Prune your schedule back if needed. Pacesetting leaders focus.

4: The "greener grass" syndrome

There's always someone smarter than you, someone prettier, or more muscular than you. There is always someone more handsome or beautiful than you perceive your partner to be. If you are not careful you can get "greener grass" syndrome. "If only my husband could be like that." "If only my wife could be like that."

Author Nancy Anderson writes,[1]

> My husband and I had one of the worst marriages I've ever seen, but now we really love each other, and even like each other! If our marriages are well-watered, the grass on our own side of the fence will be lush and soft and lovely. If you are both content and committed to your marriage, the Flirty Franks and Teasing Tinas at the office or the grocery store won't be as tempting.

Even leaders can suffer from "greener grass" syndrome, always looking for the next step in their leadership path. They might think, "I'm a manager, but if only I could be the CEO." "I'm a pastor, but if only I could be the superintendent."

A woman found out her pastor was looking at the possibility of applying to pastor at another church. So during a church service she stood up and gave a prophetic word: "Thus saith the LORD, 'I say unto thee, I knowest that thou art looking for greener pastures, but I say unto thee, the cow dung smells just as bad over there as it does here, so stay put,' saith the LORD!" That's funny, but it's also true!

There is always somebody or someplace that seems more attractive. But I tell you again, your kingdom within becomes your kingdom without. If you are having problems at your church or job, and are not resolving those problems, you will have those same problems at the next church or job or relationship. Stay in your own "pasture" until God moves you on.

5: Money, pleasure and the good life

There's nothing wrong with money, pleasure, or an enjoyable life, but the root of our faith must be firmly in the Word of God. The cares of this life and the deceitfulness of riches, not riches

---

[1] Anderson, Nancy C., *Avoiding the Greener Grass Syndrome: How to Grow Affair-Proof Hedges Around Your Marriage*, Kregel Publications, Grand Rapids, MI, 49501, 2004.

themselves, will choke out the working of the Word of God in our lives. When money or pleasure becomes the primary pursuit, a leader has gone into deceit. Jesus said the desire for other things gets us off course and into destruction.

In his book, Charles Shepard[2] chronicles the ministry scandals of the 1980s. I was fascinated to read that the root problems in these ministries was not initially sexual sin but started with the mishandling of finances. The late G. Raymond Carlson, the general superintendent of the Assemblies of God at the time, studied every minister who landed on the scrap heap and found that every one had financial mismanagement issues before any other sin. The deceitfulness of riches snared them and led them astray in evermore sinister ways.

6: Unsanctified ambition

Paul shrugged off every notion of personal ambition and self-glory. He said, "As for human praise, we have never sought it from you or anyone else."[3] Ambitious leaders desire the praise and glory of man rather than the applause of heaven. They emphasize their title and position, but a position doesn't make a leader. It is the anointing, the character, and the development of excellent leadership skills.

Unsanctified ambition has led more people into emotional exhaustion and onto the scrap heap than probably anything else. When you are always pushing in your own strength, you will one day end up on the scrap heap. When we understand God's laws and how things come into existence, we don't have to exhaust ourselves with personal, unsanctified ambition. We can let God take us where we are going.

---

[2] Shepard, Charles E., *Forgiven: The Rise and Fall of Jim Bakker and the PTL Ministry*, Atlantic Monthly Press, New York, NY, 1989.
[3] 1 Thessalonians 2:6 NLT

How do you know it's not your own personal ambition pushing you? When you let God lead and open the doors, you will be relaxed, confident and absolutely joyful. Unsanctified ambition stresses us out in all the wrong ways. The steps of a righteous man or woman—and a pacesetting leader—are ordered by the Lord. We don't need unsanctified ambition. Jesus said many will stand before the Judgment and say, "God, look at all that I've done." They had ambition, but it was their own ambition. He will say to them, "I never knew you; depart from Me."[4] These things were not ordered by the Lord for these particular people. They were doing something by unsanctified ambition rather than by the direction of the Holy Spirit.

7: The martyr syndrome

A pacesetting leader should never get into the mind-set of, "I hope everybody feels sorry for me." The leader engulfed in self-pity has left the pacesetter's path—and is simply pathetic! Nobody wants to follow someone who thinks he or she is a martyr. All you hear is, "Look how unfairly people are treating me. Look what life dealt me." The leader who is full of self-pity wants to blame someone else for everything that goes wrong. Feeling that you are a martyr separates you from your real self, from other people, from your vision, and from God. Self-pity is an enemy, but it's an enemy you don't have to choose. Don't develop the martyr syndrome.

8: Pride

Pride says to God, "That's all right. I can do it myself." Talk about self-centered rather than Christ-centered! Pride is the ulti-mate human sin, the original sin, you might say. It is choosing your own will rather than God's will, and this can be subtle. We might choose our will in a conversation, a small decision at work

---

[4] Matthew 7:23, NKJV

or while in the pulpit. All of it is pride. Whole books have been written on this subject and I encourage you to keep before you all the Scriptures about pride and arrogance. The fruit of pride is always humiliation, shame, and disgrace.

9: Self-defeating attitudes

Three of the most self-defeating attitudes on the planet are a victim mentality (the sister to self-pity), the entitlement mentality, and the scarcity mentality. Any one of these will knock you off the pacesetter's path. Don't think that everyone is against you and you are some kind of saint. Don't think you are entitled to more. And don't oppose God by thinking there isn't enough to go around. The fact is, there is an unlimited supply of everything we need—enough for every person on the planet. God has an inexhaustible supply and he knows where it is. The scarcity mentality, in particular, will suck the life out of you and turn you against his promises.

10: Violating trust

As a leader, people will come to you with problems in confidence and share things with you they don't want anyone else to know. Violating that trust is one of the most serious leadership violations. There are things I know about people that I will carry to my grave. Ministers have confided in me, and unless it's a crime, sexual molestation, or something that must be told to authorities, I *never* bring it up again. Just about the worst thing you can do is counsel someone who reveals secrets to you, then start talking about those secrets with others. I don't even bring it up as a prayer request because I don't want to violate the precious trust people place in me as their leader.

In my thirty-plus years of ministry, only two leaders have violated my confidence. One was a minister who shared a confidential file of mine. The second was a presbyter who asked how

I came to a certain conclusion about an issue we were facing. In good faith I sent him a three-page letter explaining how I came to that conclusion and some of the things I had observed. I stamped every page with "Confidential." He made several copies and disseminated then to other people!

Violating trust is so serious an offense that I believe a pastor or leader who commits this error should be pulled out of leadership. A leader has no right to lead if he or she is telling other people's confidences. Trust is number one in leadership.

Next we will look at more pitfalls—so we can avoid them!

DEVOTIONAL REFLECTIONS

1: Name three of the above pitfalls you feel especially vulnerable to as a leader.

2: How do you plan to build safeguards into your life so you can avoid ending up on the scrap heap of life in these areas?

3: Pray and ask God to reveal areas where you might be vulnerable right now and not know it.

The steps of a righteous man or woman—
and a pacesetting leader—are ordered by
the Lord.

Real leadership is about helping people fulfill their greatest potential in Christ at the workplace or in ministry or at home.

35
CHAPTER

MORE PITFALLS ON THE PACESETTER'S PATH

Remember that the Bible says the memory of the wicked will be wiped out.[1] Some of those wicked people started out on the pacesetter's path but were led astray or fell into one of these pitfalls. Let's not be one of them. We don't want our memory to be wiped out. We want our legacy and the things we have taught to go on until Jesus comes.

11: Failing to continually add value to your leadership

Leadership is about character and exceptional skills. You must keep developing new skills in leadership or you will stray from the path. The nature of God's Kingdom and of leadership is to keep moving forward to greater excellence. All of us should sincerely ask, "Lord for the sake of others, how can I add new value to my leadership? How can I bring additional value to people's lives?"

---

[1] Psalm 34:16

Real leadership is about helping people fulfill their greatest potential in Christ at the workplace or in ministry or at home. The Lord wants to continually teach you. He will show you books and resources and classes you can take to bring new skills and knowledge to your leadership. God is always giving you opportunities to add value to your life and leadership. When you do, you will multiply that value in the people you are leading.

12: Spending too much time on dark personalities

Dale Doty and Tony Cooke wrote a teaching called *Personality Disorders in the Church*. Every leader will encounter "dark personalities," but many leaders spend too much time with them and not enough with committed, solution-oriented, faithful, diligent people.

There are people in your business or church who want to help you succeed—pay the most attention to them! I wrote a book called *How to Help Your Pastor Succeed*. I could have titled it, *How to Help Your Leader Succeed*. Leaders almost always have protégés. Moses had Joshua; Elijah had Elisha; Paul had Timothy. The difference between a protégé and a parasite is that a parasite only wants to take from you to build themselves up. A true protégé wants what's in your heart. They want to become like you and carry your nature.

There are true protégés in any organization. Most of your time should be spent with them, not the dark personalities. Here are some of the dark personalities you will face as a leader:

- **Jezebel Jake: he needs to control**
- **Arrogant Absalom: I can do your job better**
- **Billy Belial: the lazy sloth**
- **The Accuser: he likes to point a finger of blame**
- **The Antagonist: always harassing people**
- **Leviathan: right about everything**

- Imagination Prophets: speaking their opinions as words from God
- Mammon Devotees: will start tithing when they win the lottery
- Movie Producer: overhears conversations and develops a scenario worthy of Hollywood
- Unteachable Know-it-all: "I know"
- The Prima Donna: "Serve me first"
- Shimei: constantly nipping at your heels
- Sanballat & Tobiah: anti-progress, against every new idea
- Delusional Private: believes he's a five-star general; never learned the concept of authority
- The Pharisee: religious and demanding
- The Committee Man: every issue resolved by committee
- The Verizon Vixen: he or she keeps the satellites burning with the latest juicy gossip
- Church Mafia: conspire to have their way and make threats if they don't get it. "I'm concerned that if you don't do this, we're going to have to withhold our tithe."
- The "Me" Saint: "I'm not being fed. I don't like the music. I don't like the lighting. I don't like this, I don't like that."
- Chatty Cathy: talks forever about nothing
- Tall Poppy: "I want you blessed, just not more than me!"
- Twisted Twirlies: like those ice cream cones that are chocolate and vanilla twirled together, this personality is twisted in their thinking and personality. You can say something sincerely and

positively, even give a Scripture verse, and they twist it somehow.

You might also run into Scarcity Scarecrow, Entitlement Teddy and Victim Victor. But the most dangerous personality of all is—you! Because only you can decide who your circle of friends will be. Only you can decide if you will spend your time with those who are committed to lifting up the vision and working toward the goals, or if you will spend your time on the dark personalities that aren't going to have a positive influence on your organization or church.

My advice is to develop the skill of walking away kindly. Be kind, but walk away from these people. Give your time to those who are taking your church, your business, your ministry, your family toward the vision God has given.

13: Carelessness in morals

This is Samson's story. He was raised up to be Israel's deliverer.[2] Instead he spent his time making up riddles and lusting after foreign girls. Finally, because of his lust, he lost it all. The enemy gouged out his eyes and took him into bondage. Yes, his last act was heroic, but he died to perform it.

Paul said...

1 Thessalonians 5:22
Abstain from all appearance of evil."

For a pacesetting leader, there should be no question about your morals. Go far out of your way to avoid even the hint of impropriety and wrongdoing.

A young pastor got a telephone call from a woman who was at a motel and needed counseling. He said, "I can't come there and counsel you."

---

[2] Judges 13

She said, "I'm going to commit suicide if you don't!" Burdened by the thought of her taking her life, he went to the motel and met her in the parking lot.

"I've got groceries in the car," she said. "Would you help me carry them in?" He carried them in, and though he did nothing wrong just walking into the hotel with her, the act did not *appear* innocent. He was seen by a member of his church, and it created awful problems for him. That pastor was careless and not concerned with avoiding the appearance of evil.

If you're a leader meeting with someone of the opposite sex, the door should stay open the width of a hand. Do not ride in a vehicle with someone of the opposite sex. Always have someone else in the car with you. That way if there is ever gossip about you, you will be able to prove it's not true.

These are just a few of the rules you should put in place, and most of them are just common sense. Set strong personal boundaries. Don't think you're above temptation, and don't give anyone else reason to question your moral integrity.

14: Trying to advance without adequate preparation

There are qualifications for leadership. Some people launch a business without taking the time to prepare a business plan. They have no philosophy of leadership. They try to get to home plate while skipping second base or third base. However, as we know, even a home run doesn't count unless you touch *all* the bases.

When I was young, I was not prepared for ministry, but I thought I was. I mentioned how I put out four-color literature and waited for my phone to ring. I practically went broke publishing that beautiful literature. Not one telephone call came, and now I'm glad! I wasn't prepared. I might have destroyed my ministry before it even got off the ground.

God will open doors when your preparation and his opportunities meet. Don't try to advance beyond your preparation.

15: Negativity

A pacesetting leader must stand against disorder and sin, but denouncing evil without balancing your message with grace, mercy, and hope will lead to your downfall. We all know certain types that are critical all the time. You get around them and you know it's going to be a negative experience. "Did you read the news today? It's all bad!" they say.

Negativism in leadership is magnified much more. It cripples and corrodes the human spirit. It shows a lack of trust in God. Negativity has no value to a leader. When a leader is secure and confident, he or she speaks the truth in love but is never needlessly negative. People will look up to you, respect you, honor you, and treasure you for not being infected by the negativity so rampant in the world.

Leaders infected by negativism are broken people. They cannot advance because of their poisonous, toxic attitude. God will not give them more until they are free of it. Negativity nets nothing. You will never lead properly or influence anyone for good with negativity. It's an ill-fitting attitude for a leader.

16: Laziness

Leaders who are disinclined to work or exert themselves have not only left the pacesetter's path, they are taking a nap on the side of the road! Balance your checkbook. Make your business plan. Do your reports. Do your taxes. Cut the weeds. Get the jobs done.

Proverbs 6:10–11 NKJV
[10] A little sleep, a little slumber, A little folding of the hands to sleep—
[11] So shall your poverty come on you like a prowler, And your need like an armed man.

Now, on to the rest of the pitfalls we need to watch out for.

DEVOTIONAL REFLECTIONS

1: Which of these pitfalls have you seen people fall into?

2: To which are you most vulnerable?

3: Write down two or three pitfalls from this chapter and briefly say how you will avoid them.

The failure to study is a major pitfall on the pacesetters path.

36
CHAPTER

FINAL PITFALLS ON THE PACESETTER'S PATH

Let's look at these final pitfalls in the pacesetter's path.

17: Wrong methods of fund raising

This warning is especially for leaders in nonprofit and ministry settings. There are so many gimmicks that ministries are tempted to use. One minister sent out the "Miracle Scarlet Thread," claiming it was like the miracle scarlet rope that hung from Rahab's house that protected her from danger. He sent the scarlet thread out with a note that said, "I'm going to pray over this scarlet thread when you send it back to me with your generous donation. When you hang that scarlet thread out your window the way Rahab hung the scarlet rope out her window, it will protect you."

How about miracle wallets? I've seen them with my own eyes. Ministers raise funds by sending out cardboard miracle wallets printed so they look like they're made of leather. You are supposed to put your generous offering in the miracle wallet, send it back and the evangelist will pray over it. Then he will send the miracle wallet back after he takes out your generous gift, and that miracle wallet supposedly will never go empty. It will bring you an endless supply.

It's amazing how gullible some people are. When I received that miracle wallet in the mail I thought, "If he's got all these miracle wallets that produce a never-ending supply, rather than asking me for a generous donation, why doesn't he go to the warehouse where they keep all those miracle wallets and get all the money he needs?"

I have seen miracle wheat, holy water, miracle water and one of the funniest ones, the holy spot. That was an 11 x 17 piece of paper with a big yellow spot in the middle called the holy spot. You were supposed to kneel on the holy spot, write your prayer requests on the holy spot and send it back with your generous donation. The evangelist would pray that all the prayers you prayed while you were on the holy spot would come true.

The worst one I ever saw was the holy shower cap. I am not kidding. It had a picture of the evangelist's hand on top of the shower cap. You sent the shower cap back with your offering, he would pray over it and you would wear it for twenty-four hours with a picture of his hand on top as if he were praying for you. If only I were joking!

God gave us methods for raising money in his Word: tithes, offerings, alms, faith promises and first fruits. Don't be afraid to teach those methods and practice them.

18: Doctrinal sidetracks

This, too, is especially for leaders in ministry, but it has a business application as well. Don't get sidetracked by useless theorizing that has no real-world benefit. I remember listening to a message by a teacher talking about demons. He was telling the audience, "Some of you have demons of anger. Some of you have demons of lust and demons of this and of that. You all brought brown paper bags. When I give the command, vomit the demon into the bag!" Then he said, "All right, come out, demons." I could hear all this gagging. I thought, "Gagging out demons into a little brown bag! Then what do you do with the bag? Give it to somebody you don't like?"

The pacesetter's path doesn't have a lot of novel teachings on it. The Gospel of God's Kingdom is very plain. Most business strategies are the same way. Avoid spending time on unfruitful, exotic questions and ideas.

19: Failure to study

Some never rise above mediocrity because they watch seven hours of mindless television every day and do not study to improve their leadership.[1] We saw in an earlier chapter how study is critical in a pacesetting leader's preparation.

20: Poor counsel

When I was a young minister, the only people who came to me with unsolicited advice were those whom I did not want to emulate. When people come to you with advice, look at their lives, their situation, their ministry, their business. Ask yourself, "Do I really want to accept advice from this person?" Accepting poor advice can land you on the scrap heap.

21: Sectarianism

If you shut out other people and cling to the idea of "We four and no more," you have become sectarian. Jesus rebuked the disciples for sectarianism. They said, "Somebody was casting out devils in your name, and we stopped him because he's not part of our group!" Jesus said, "If he's not against us, he's for us. Let him go cast out devils in my Name."[2]

[1] 2 Timothy 2:15
[2] Mark 9

This is true in business, too, when you develop a culture of superiority and you refuse to let "outsiders" influence or even join you. Don't shut out other people just because they are not like you. Chances are that God sent them to you so you would learn something new!

Joe Robbe is a graduate of the Pacesetting Leadership Course and is now the pastor of Mount Hope Church in Portland, Michigan. Joe is amazing. He took a church that was in debt, had one member, had fallen apart physically, and had a bad name in the community. It's now a flourishing church and has been doing great for more than twenty years. How?

One of the main reasons for Joe's success is that he listened to the Lord about building relationships with other pastors in Portland. Instead of seeing new pastors as competition, he sees them as reinforcements! He joined the local ministerial association of pastors and has been the president of that association for the last several years. They get together twice a month to pray for each other's churches and needs and to plan community prayer events. Joe and those pastors have a Kingdom mind-set. They are not exclusive but inclusive, open, and welcoming.

I recently asked Joe about it and he said, "The unity we have as pastors flows down and permeates all our congregations. We have a love and appreciation for one another. It wasn't like that when I got here, but over time the spirit of cooperation has grown. It has had a positive influence and contributed to a very healthy spiritual atmosphere here."

Joe told me recently that the pacesetting leadership course transformed his life. He likes how it's down-to-earth and practical, and he offers the course at his church to train new leaders. I like the way Joe demonstrates pacesetting leadership in real life!

22: Making excuses for your failures

All leaders make mistakes. We all will do something that just doesn't work out the way we thought it would. I wish I could say it was different, but it's not. The best thing you can do is analyze your failures, seek advice from a trusted friend or mentor, or find a book or teaching that offers God's wisdom. But the first thing you do is accept responsibility. Don't blame circumstances or other people. Take the blame and move on. People respect that and it builds integrity in you and others.

23: Failing to enjoy life and make leadership enjoyable

I remember being at a prayer meeting when God spoke to my heart, "Prophesy life, laughter, and love over this church." That was an unusual word, but it was exactly what we needed! Your organization should be a fun place. As a leader, make your ministry or business environment enjoyable. Set a merry, cheerful tone even as you take on big plans and projects. Enjoy the work and the people around you, give compliments, and have a sunny demeanor. Then you will reflect God's nature, and the people around you will thrive.

24: Failing to develop enthusiasm

When your church or business is enthusiastic, more people will follow. Enthusiasm will give you a glow that spills over to others. Don't be a drone with a negative tone. If God has given you a vision, celebrate that by your attitude. Celebrate it with your words. Speak publicly about it.

The disciples went out and told the things they saw and heard, which were astonishing. You should do the same thing. Mention it wherever you go. Even if people react in a hostile way, you're imparting something to them. Seeds will go into the ground and someday bear fruit.

Enthusiasm will make you radiant. One night a church was on fire and the volunteer fire department came to put it out. Standing nearby was Charlie, who never went to church.

Someone said, "Charlie, I've never seen you at church before."

He replied, "That's because I've never seen the church on fire before!" You should be on fire with enthusiasm for whatever it is you do!

25: Giving up too quickly

Jesus gave an amazing parable about the sower and the seed. "

Matthew 13:3–8, NKJV

³ Then He spoke many things to them in parables, saying: "Behold, a sower went out to sow.

⁴ And as he sowed, some seed fell by the wayside; and the birds came and devoured them.

⁵ Some fell on stony places, where they did not have much earth; and they immediately sprang up because they had no depth of earth.

⁶ But when the sun was up they were scorched, and because they had no root they withered away.

⁷ And some fell among thorns, and the thorns sprang up and choked them.

⁸ But others fell on good ground and yielded a crop: some a hundredfold, some sixty, some thirty.

The point? Keep sowing that seed! In this story the farmer lost seventy-five percent of his seed to birds, thorns, and the scorching sun. But the seed that took root produced a whole lot more than he sowed and more than made up for the loss.

Most people give up too soon. Persistence, even through the hard times, shows a strength of character that you need as a leader. Pastors, for example, have an average tenure of about three and a half years, but research shows that they become most effective only after six years. If they dig in their heels and stick with it—even in the face of frustration and momentary failure—they will find success on the pacesetter's path. Persistence and faith work together.

DEVOTIONAL REFLECTIONS

1: Which of the 25 pitfalls on the pacesetter's path do you feel most applies to you?

2: What is the most important idea you have taken away from this message?

As a pacesetting leader you will leave a lasting legacy as you study and apply God's leadership principles.

37
CHAPTER

A FINAL WORD

More than thirty years ago, Mary Jo and I were on our way to a meeting in Detroit when we stopped at a place called John's Pancake House. We were excited that morning because we knew God had called us to ministry. We didn't know where the path would take us, but we knew that our steps would be ordered by the Lord.

As we were talking about our future and about ministry, I said, "Mary Jo, whatever we do, God is going to make us successful and fruitful! We are going to succeed in everything we do!" It was an exciting realization, and it has proven true.

We went off to that meeting in Detroit, and when we got back I made a 3 x 5 card that said, "In Jesus' name, I'm going to succeed in everything I do." I signed my name to it and posted it in my home. Every day I saw that affirmation, that declaration, that faith announcement. I repeated it to myself, "In Jesus' name, I'm going to succeed in everything I do." The power was in Jesus' name, not on my own.

Success simply means fruitfulness in God's Kingdom. Authentic success has no ambition or pride in it. It bears his fruit in his timing. God has called you to succeed as a leader. He has called you to be fruitful in everything you put your hand to in his plan. He has called you to lead right where you are—in your community, your church, the marketplace, the nonprofit sector, the homeowner's association, the chamber of commerce, in your family, and with your friends. As a pacesetting leader, you will leave a lasting legacy as you study and apply God's leadership principles.

My prayer is that God will give you exceptional opportunities, that he will show you how to develop an extraordinary faith and tenacity that will bring to your life remarkable productivity. I pray, through the name of Jesus and by the power of the Holy Spirit, that God will fill you with uncommon anointing and ability. That you will use your anointing and abilities effectively as a pacesetting leader, bringing glory to God wherever you go and wherever you have influence.

Now lead!

TESTIMONIES FROM PACESETTING LEADERSHIP COURSE GRADUATES

PASTOR JOHN GALLINETTI: MOUNT HOPE CHURCH, GRAND BLANC, MI

www.mhcgb.com

We started with eight people in my basement in 1988. Today we have 1,100 people and are in a massive building project.

Our church and everyone's involvement is based on the teaching found in pacesetting leadership. It is powerful. The truths and precepts communicated from those principles set the pace for people to understand how we function here. A servant's heart, a teachable attitude, an increasing desire to draw closer to Jesus—we communicate each one of those as part of the school of the Bible here. People have to go through the class to be involved in our church.

I just got done teaching my twenty-fifth Pacesetting Leadership class since we planted the church in 1988. We could not be doing what we've done here without the instruction from pacesetting leadership. It is so good. Right thinking is so important, especially when it comes to believers developing their faith. Many people in the business world love it. They take it and implement it in their businesses. People find out they are gifted in a way to release that gifting in the local church. It lets you know you're not just a number, but you are here for a reason and a purpose.

These pacesetting leadership principles are a revelation for people. It's so much fun to teach every year because the teacher learns more than the pupil. The whole course and book is interwoven in our lives. We couldn't do ministry without it. If I were to go somewhere else, I would implement pacesetting leadership immediately. We've got teams who come from other churches to take the class. It changes people in the pew. We see a lot of people going from doing nothing to being great volunteers or leading a small group. They go from being synthetic to authentic. They develop a sparkling, faith-filled attitude that is exemplified here.

ANTHONY YEBOAH: MISSIONARY TO WEST AFRICA

www.freeinternationalmissions.com

Pacesetting leadership has been a huge blessing. I trained at the Mount Hope Bible Training Institute and finished in 1991. Pacesetting leadership was part of the curriculum. I read it over and over and over. The moment I graduated, I started a Bible school in Africa which is now a four-year college that has graduated almost 750 pastors. We used *The Art of Pacesetting Leadership* as part of our curriculum. With that we have planted 317 churches in different African countries. In 2006, they made me a bishop over 3,000 pastors in Ivory Coast.

I brought the president of Burundi to speak to pastors in Grand Rapids last year. I have worked with the president of Nigeria and the president of Ethiopia to build orphanages. We are helping

Burundi build schools. Pacesetting leadership has been used in most of what we have done. It has helped me to be a good leader in everything you think about as a leader. Testimonies from our pastors say they learn basic things they think they already know but actually don't. If you practice the principles of pacesetting leadership it not only helps you but your church. For business men and women it has been a great help. I am in business, too, and I use these same principles with my workers.

I didn't go to any school apart from the Bible Training Institute, but I got hold of the principles and put them into practice and it took me where I am today. I saw what God had done through Dave, and I always believed that God would do through me what he had done for Dave. Pacesetting leadership gave me the vision of how to do it.

PASTOR NORM OBERLIN: MOUNT HOPE CHURCH, GAYLORD MI

www.gaylordchurch.com

Barb and I had trained under Pastor Dave Williams before we went to Bible college. We always say that most of the hands-on training we received was from Dave and *The Art of Pacesetting Leadership*. We felt so far ahead of our fellow students. In college they only gave us book knowledge. Pastor Dave gave us the practical stuff that we really could use.

We offer the *The Art of Pacesetting Leadership* course at our church. Many of our people had never been introduced to that kind of teaching. But once people started to take pacesetting leadership, they realized it helps them not just at church but in business, at home, and in their relationship with the Lord.

I think it helps people to realize that they can be leaders. So many of us are naturally put in leadership positions, even as parents, but don't consider what that means.

This course gives us the tools to be better leaders. It teaches us that you must be a humble servant. I've been in full-time ministry for over twenty years, I and haven't seen anything out there that equips people as well as *The Art of Pacesetting Leadership*. Three of my boys have gone through the course, and I believe it's one of the reasons they're in ministry today.

KERBY RIALS: AOG MISSIONARY TO RUSSIA

I was the first to translate the *The Art of Pacesetting Leadership* course into the Russian language. The bishop in the Russian province of Kaliningrad made it required for all their pastors to study. That was quite a compliment. The thing about pacesetting leadership that I, and the Russians, like is that it's practical and accessible. It breaks down the elements of leadership into components that are easily understood and grounded in the Bible. It prepares people and pastors to understand what godly leadership is and how to support their leaders. It builds a structure into a church that is essential if a church is going to advance. If you have division, rebellion, or lazy workers the church will never grow. Pacesetting leadership addresses all those issues clearly.

PASTOR JOE ROBBE: MOUNT HOPE CHURCH, PORTLAND MI

www.portlandmounthope.org

When I came to Mount Hope Church in Lansing, it was a pivotal time in my life. I sensed a call to ministry, but didn't know what to do. I had experienced deep hurts and felt confused.

It wasn't until 1988 that things changed. I took *The Art of Pacesetting Leadership* course. Halfway through, the call to ministry that had been covered by hurts and wounds, rose up with clarity. The teaching helped me to identify and answer the call. Those two months cleared up eleven years of uncertainty and transformed my life.

I like that *The Art of Pacesetting Leadership* is a very down-to-earth, "where the rubber meets the road" teaching for leadership and ministry. I have taught it at my church, and we incorporated it into our leadership training. Pastor Dave Williams has been the most influential person in my life as a mentor and role model. The class and book have been instrumental in my life as an individual and as a pastor. I use it on a regular basis. It's relevant and easy to apply. It's also part of the building block of classes our members go through.

Pastors from every denomination have a great relationship in Portland. Some of the teaching I've gotten from Dave has really helped me in my view and attitude toward other pastors and churches. I am the president of our local ministerial association. I see new pastors not as competition but as reinforcements. I got that attitude from Dave. He said, "If someone wanted to build a church next door, I would give them my blessing and see what I could do to help them." That is God's Kingdom mind-set.

Pacesetting leadership principles have had a positive influence and contributed to a very healthy spiritual atmosphere in Portland. I know they will work for your life and ministry too!

Contact Information

Dave Williams Ministries
P.O. Box 80825
Lansing, MI 48908-0825

For a complete list of Dave Williams'
life-changing books,
audio messages, and videos visit our website:

www.davewilliams.com

or phone:
800-888-7284
or
517-731-0000

About Dave Williams, D.Min.

America's Pacesetting Life Coach™

Dave is a popular speaker at rallies, minister's conferences, churches, civic group meetings, business training sessions, colleges, camps and Bible Schools. He coaches church leaders, business leaders, entrepreneurs, and followers of Christ on how to live a pacesetting life. His three-pronged approach—spiritual, attitudinal, and practical—has transformed ordinary people into extraordinarily successful leaders in every field of endeavor.

Through cultivating the individual's inherent gifts and enhancing professional—or ministry—performance, he helps to instill the kind of authentic values that attract success. He emphasizes that staying connected to the Great Commission will ultimately lead to greater levels of accomplishment.

BEST SELLING AUTHOR

Dave has authored over 60 books that teach and inspire readers in Christian growth, financial success, health and healing, and many other areas of Christian living. His book *The New Life... The Start of Something Wonderful* has sold almost three million copies and has been translated into eight languages. More recently, he wrote *The World Beyond* (over 100,000 copies sold).

His *Miracle Results of Fasting* (Harrison House Publishers) was an Amazon.com five-star top seller for two years in a row.

Dave's articles and reviews have appeared in national magazines such as *Advance, Pentecostal Evangel, Charisma, Ministries Today, Lansing Magazine, Detroit Free Press, World News*, and others.

Dave Williams served as pastor of Mount Hope Church in Lansing, Michigan, for more than thirty years. In that time, Dave trained thousands of ministers through the Mount Hope Bible Training Institute, Dave Williams' Church Planter's School, and Dave Williams' School for Pacesetting Church Leaders.

With the help of his staff and partners, Dave established a 72-acre campus with worship center, Bible Training Institute, children's center, Global Prayer Center, Valley of Blessing, Gilead Healing Center, care facilities, event center, café, fitness center, world evangelism headquarters, Global Communications Center, and an office complex with nine buildings.

Church planting and missions have been a focus for Dave Williams. Under his leadership, 43 new Mount Hope Churches were planted in the United States, over 300 in West Africa, South Africa, Zimbabwe, and 200 in Asia with a combined membership exceeding 80,000 people. During Dave's tenure, Mount Hope Church gave over $40,000,000 to world and local missions.

Today, Dave serves as the global ambassador and "Bishop" for Mount Hope Churches. He also leads Strategic Global Mission (for charitable scholarships and grants), Dave Williams Ministries, Club 52 (for business people and entrepreneurs), and The Pacesetting Life Media Ministries.

Dave served as a national general presbyter for the Assemblies of God, assistant district superintendent, executive presbyter, regent for North Central Bible College (now North Central University), and as a national missions board member.

PACESETTING PRODUCTS
TO ACCELERATE YOUR SUCCESS

The Miracle of Faith Goals

This book reveals God's Plan for accomplishing great things. You will learn the seven "Vs", incremental steps, that will help you accomplish 100 to 1000 times more!

135 PAGES

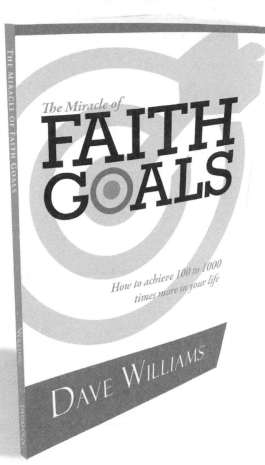

Select titles available on:

amazonkindle nook *by Barnes & Noble* iBooks

WWW.DECAPOLISPUBLISHING.COM
1-800-888-7284

Your Spectacular Mind

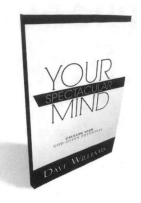

Your thoughts create your environment. If you want a better life, you need better thinking. In this book, Dave Williams unlocks the mysteries of the mind, giving you plans and strategies for developing your mind—an awesome gift from God.

108 PAGES

How to Help Your Pastor Succeed

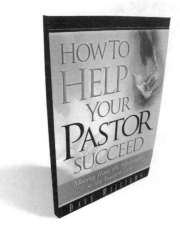

In over 30 years of successful ministry, Dave Williams has developed proven methods to assist you in helping your pastor and church succeed. You will learn: how to move to the inner circle, enforce Christ's victory in your city, spot and discern wolves, and many other strategies for supporting your pastor.

PN8038—197 PAGES

Private Garden
Tender Prophetic Words to Encourage You

In over 30 years of successful ministry. Dave Williams has experienced both triumphs and trials. But at all times—and in all circumstances—the Holy Spirit has been faithful to comfort and sustain him.

220 PAGES

Turning Ordinary Talks Into Heavenly Impartations Seminar

This seminar shows you how to motivate and inspire your listeners. It will lead you to an understanding of how to pursue God's anointing so you not only inform and instruct but also impart something from heaven.

2 MESSAGES & WORKBOOK

CD Sets

Creating Your New Reality

8 MESSAGES

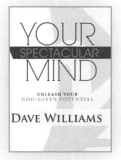

Your Spectacular Mind

2 MESSAGES

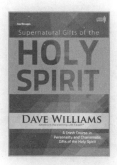

Supernatural Gifts of the Holy Spirit

4 MESSAGES

Ebooks

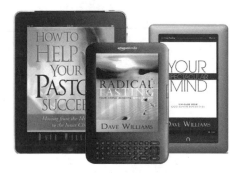

Kindle, Nook, and iBooks

Many titles are available for your e-reader!

- ° Skill For Battle
- ° The Imposter
- ° Road to Radical Riches
- ° Upward
- ° And more!

Check your ebook store for prices and easy downloads.